the key to success
Aase Pethle

THE MANAGER'S GUIDE TO SERVICE EXCELLENCE

THE MANAGER'S GUIDE TO SERVICE EXCELLENCE

☆ ☆ ☆ ☆ ☆

The Fine Art of Customer Service

Anne Petite

SUMMERHILL PRESS

© 1989 Anne Petite

Published by
Summerhill Press Ltd., Toronto, M5T 1A2

Distributed in Canada by
University of Toronto Press, 5201 Dufferin Street,
Downsview, Ontario M3H 5T8

Distributed in the United States by
Sterling Publishing, 387 Park Avenue South,
New York, New York, 10016-8810

Cover design by
Images Art Direction and Design Inc.
Text design
by Michelle Maynes

Canadian Cataloguing in Publication Data
Petite, Anne, (Date)
The manager's guide to service excellence
Includes index.
ISBN 0-920197-69-8
1. Customer service. I. Title.

HF5415.5.P47 1989   658.8'12   C89-094278-1

Printed and bound in the United States

To Chesley

CONTENTS

Preface

The message from customers is clear: deliver service or we will take our business elsewhere. In contemporary business practices, customer satisfaction must be recognized as a priority which contributes to any organization's competitive advantage.

The Manager's Guide to Service Excellence: The Fine Art of Customer Service, is for business people who care about their customers and how those customers are treated every day, by everyone in the company. It is designed to spark ideas and stimulate discussion as well as to encourage both managers and staff to look at service from the customer's point of view. The anecdotes throughout the book all illustrate everyday service situations. As well, there are practical suggestions for service improvement that are applicable to most organizations or departments. At the end of each chapter, the "Take a Break... Time Out" pages present ideas for dealing with specific aspects of service. The questions included in these sections are designed to encourage managers — and staff — to evaluate the service their company or department offers from the customer's standpoint.

The three questions at the beginning of each chapter are critical to the delivery of quality service. The answer "Yes" to each of the questions is the difference between talk and action.

This book is the result of several years of experience in consulting and training in customer service with my associate, Ruth Haehnel. We have worked with a wide variety of organizations, each of which has one thing in common — senior people who know the importance of service to the financial bottom-line and who are committed to taking active roles in service improvement.

My thanks to all the people mentioned who took time from busy schedules to talk with me about their service policies and practices. The companies they represent all regard quality service as essential business practice. Their contributions provide valuable and relevant illustrations of practical situations and solutions.

My thanks as well to Stanley Skinner who not only encouraged me to write this book, but suggested the direction to take.

CHAPTER 1

SERVICE

The "S" in Success

☐ UNDERSTOOD?
☐ ACCEPTED?
☐ PART OF DAILY PRACTICE?

Service: The Foundation of
Customer Confidence

A generation ago, people took service for granted. It was assumed that companies, shops, and banks wanted your business and were prepared to make you feel a valued customer. Now good service is something to be treasured when you find it, and is frequently an additional cost. From the business point of view, service is often regarded as an add-on and is scrutinized under cost/benefit analysis. With this attitude, something has been lost, something directly affecting the quality of business and life.

If you put together all the changes that have happened over the last few decades — social, economic, environmental — you have situations and pressures for which there are no precedents. The rate of change in every aspect of life is both disquieting and exciting, creating entirely new circumstances and conditions.

Frequently today, service seems to be considered more as a nuisance than as an essential business practice, with bottom-line implications. Many people at all levels, including those in positions of responsibility, don't seem to have a grasp of the meaning of service either as a concept or as a practice.

Service is often bandied around in business discussions as a motherhood word, assumed to be desirable, but difficult to define in objective terms. Most people can describe in detail the occasions when they haven't had service, and they always remember when service has been truly extraordinary, but they can't give you a step-by-step analysis of the good service habits that make business flow smoothly, day by day.

On social occasions, when people find out that I'm a consultant in customer service, they immediately tell me their latest service horror stories. I am regaled with anecdotes about the inferior service at an expensive restaurant, the time spent waiting in line at the ticket counter, a half hour wait beyond the scheduled appointment in the doctor's office, an order incorrectly filled, a major business purchase that did not meet the specs, errors in billing.... The variety of these experiences is unlimited. But as the stories unfold, one fundamental truth is revealed: the buyer of the product or service has been disappointed, inconvenienced, and dissatisfied. Customer cynicism rather than customer confidence prevails.

The delivery of quality service today is a modern problem. Modern because rapid technological changes, rationalization, and globalization, all create situations for which there is no past history, contributing to a learn-as-you-go environment.

Unlike the past, when the shop proprietor stood at the back of the store and personally directed operations, businesses today are often large and depersonalized. Service becomes a catch-all term for unspecified actions that someone else ought to be doing. As a customer, how often have you heard, "That's the order department's problem," or "That's an accounts problem" and so on?

Although the challenge of quality service is very much a contemporary issue, one service principle has never changed: service is a transaction between people, not between companies or departments. The implications of this statement are both horrendously complicated and elegantly simple. Complicated, because you are dealing with a thousand and one variations of interaction between people. Simple, because people want only one thing — a feeling of satisfaction with the service they have received.

People dealing with people as a basic service precept applies in any business transaction, whether you are at the mega-million level, or the dollars and cents level of the every-day consumer.

Regardless of the obstacles you have to overcome, satisfactory service is whatever makes your customers feel comfortable with your product and with the action your company will take on their behalf. It's called building customer confidence.

Customer confidence evolves as a result of the consistently smooth interaction of people and systems. Satisfied customers are blissfully unaware of the behind-the-scenes actions required to deliver the meal, train the staff, print the forms, or manufacture the product. No crises, no aggravations, no discomfort.

Customers want to feel comfortable — satisfied with your service and product. But as with any elegant, simple principle, the practice isn't easy. The rules of good service have to be learned, the skills understood and practiced daily. They are not taught in schools, colleges, or universities, and judging from the horror stories about poor service that you hear all around you, the practice of service is not something that comes naturally to most of us.

When you receive excellent service, it's something to remember. The day my friend walked into a shoe store and the saleswoman remembered her shoe size, as well as the style of shoe she had bought three months before, she was astounded and thrilled. She felt as though she were an important person, a valued customer — and certainly much more than an 8 1/2 narrow with money to spend. Now when she needs shoes, where does she start? Right there, of course. It is not an inexpensive store, but she feels confident that she will be well served.

That salesperson is a service professional. She understands the basics of good service and good business: people want to feel comfortable and valued as customers;

they want to be treated as people, not potential dollars.

People dealing with people is what service is all about. We all want to feel that a person somewhere in the organization cares about our business. As impersonal technology takes over so many routine functions, such as billing, order-taking, mailing, and banking, we want to sense the personal link that makes us feel more than an invoice number.

The mother of a friend of mine ran a very successful small retail business for many years, and is now retired. When banking machines were first introduced, she received and used the card to do her banking transactions — until the day the machine accidentally swallowed her card and she discovered that there were no human beings on the other side.

"When I put my money somewhere, I want to know someone is taking responsibility for it. I'll deal with the people, not their machines," she said as she tore up the replaced card.

Simplistic? Perhaps. But whenever we tell this story in workshops, people smile a little smile of recognition and identification with my friend's mother.

Service and the Bottom Line

In one of our customer service seminars, we were talking with a group of business owners about the relationship of customer comfort and confidence to customer service.

"Comfortable!" exclaimed one of the business owners. "I have a business to run. Comfortable is what we feel when we go home at night and relax in front of the TV. What do you mean, people to people? That's not business language!"

We asked him to consider the bottom-line implications: when customers have any degree of discomfort, such as feelings of anger, fear, frustration, or bewilderment, your business with them is in a danger zone. On the other hand, customers who feel secure and comfortable dealing with your product and your staff have confidence in you and the way you do business. They perceive that the way your staff treats them is fair and reasonable. These customers are more likely to stay your customers, and this has considerable impact on the bottom line.

People dealing with people: whether it's buying a pair of shoes or a tank car of petroleum products, we all need to know there's a human being looking after our interests — a person who will treat us as more than an invoice number, who will recognize that as customers, we too have stresses, deadlines, and a need to be understood and respected.

"Yes," the business owner responded, "that all sounds very warm and cosy, but, as I have said, I do have a business to run. I don't have time to do all that soft stuff. What my customers want is the goods delivered on time, at a fair price, in good condition."

"Exactly so. That's a critical aspect of quality service," we explained. "Then you have to ensure the second step. When you are in business, getting customers is important, and *keeping* them is even more so. How you treat them makes the difference. The minutes spent honing the service skills of your people could be money in the bank. It's a blue chip investment in customer comfort and confidence."

We then gave him some bottom-line results of improved customer service:

- Increased numbers of orders and decreased numbers of complaints, as a result of increased customer satisfaction.

- Fewer errors in documentation such as order taking

and billing, as a result of improved staff awareness of customer needs.

- Decreased long distance charges, as a result of fewer call backs having to be made.

- Significant decrease in time needed and spent obtaining routine information from customers, as a result of improved communications between staff and customers.

The business owner had to agree these were bottom-line results, and for the rest of the session he was an interested participant.

You and Your Customers: A Dynamic Partnership

Think about a day in your company. Customers come in person or call on the telephone, make inquiries, request information, place orders. Each time someone in the company responds to a customer, from the initial reception to the final words, the company's business and profits hang in the balance. That is because every time customers contact anyone in your company, they form an opinion about the way you do business. The staff person who takes part in the dialogue creates an image of the way the company treats and regards customers. Each contact provides an experience for the customer — good, bad, or neutral. One contact may create a one and only mental picture of the organization's business practices. Whether or not customers feel comfortable and confident depends entirely on the quality of the contact and their perception of the experience.

You have no idea what the customers' perceptions are unless they tell you or take their business elsewhere. In other words, your customers' repeat business often depends on their perception of how they are treated by your staff. That's a very fragile link on which to maintain business, especially if staff are given no guidance on how to respond to customers.

The busy staff person, with rush orders, deadlines, and personal stresses, often has difficulty responding to every customer in a manner that carries the implicit message, "Mr. or Ms. Customer, you are my only concern at this time." But busy as he or she might be, that staff person has all the service responsibility at that moment, and is accountable for customer confidence.

Of course, a quality product is a critical component of successful business. But you need to establish the bond of partnership that creates customer confidence. The *time spent* with staff explaining, developing, and honing the service skills necessary to building that type of relationship is an *investment* in good business practices. Quality service combines partnership with customer confidence.

POSITIVE CUSTOMER PERCEPTIONS

- "This company cares about my time — their staff doesn't keep me waiting and they return my calls."
- "This company is staffed by people who are competent — they know where to find answers to my questions."
- "This company understands me and my business — they ask questions to make certain I've got what I need."
- "The staff always seem glad to hear from me — they always listen to what I have to say, even if I'm critical."
- "Everyone in this company takes time to get the facts from me the first time. My orders are always taken accurately."
- "Everyone in this company is professional — they are all excellent representatives of a good company with good products. They sound proud of their jobs and their company."
- "These people value me and my business — I have confidence in the company, the product, the staff."
- "My orders are always on time — this company really takes care of their customers!"

When you hear these kinds of comments from your customers, you have reason to be pleased. You know you are providing quality service.

Creating a Service Statement

Building customer confidence is a day-by-day process. Once you accept the fact that each customer contact is critical to customer confidence, you realize how thoughtfully and professionally you and your staff must respond to customers. You and your staff need to understand and be committed to the care and nurturing of all customers. If nurturing sounds too much like motherhood, remember the first requirement for confidence is comfort. Anyone who is mentally or physically uncomfortable is not going to give you their hearts or their minds or their dollars.

With this in mind, create a service statement for staff that will reflect your philosophy that customer comfort and confidence are critical to the health of your business. Then circulate this statement in your department or company so that each staff member is aware of the philosophy behind the business. Below is a sample service statement.

A SERVICE STATEMENT

"Our products and our services are geared to meet our customers' needs, either in their businesses or in their personal lives.

Every contact our customers have with our company or department will help them to be effective and efficient in their own businesses or personal lives.

Any time our customers contact us, over the telephone, face-to-face, or by letter, they will feel that our staff and our products serve them well. They will know we value their business and will continue to give us their business."

A service statement explains and elaborates an operating principle. The operating principle I've suggested in chapter 9 makes customer satisfaction a top priority goal. By using a statement such as the one above for all staff, you are emphasizing the importance of customer satisfaction. All staff must understand the implications of the statement and know its application to their own jobs.

Both words and actions of staff must support the underlying philosophy of the statement. When words and actions are contradictory, customers may experience the following:

- We are told when we buy a product, "Call us any time you have a question, or need assistance"... then we are put on hold for what seems an eternity.

- We buy because a selling feature is quality... then we receive a defective order.

- We're told that technical support will be available any time... then the technical person responds with impatience when we don't understand.

We talk about technology and progress, but not about people and how they feel — yet emotions are prime motivators. People will buy your product or service based on how they feel about you, your company, your product, your price. They'll continue to do business with you if they continue to *feel* confident — and comfortable.

- A public organization asks for community involvement... then schedules community meetings at hours that are inconvenient for working people who live in the community.

With a well-designed service philosophy and statement, and a clear understanding on the part of your staff of its application to daily functions, these situations can be prevented. To maintain quality service and customer confidence, you must locate sources of potential or present customer discomfort, and ask yourself (and your customers) how you can better meet the needs of those customers.

Distinguishing Wants from Needs

Customer satisfaction results when your service fulfils customers' needs and wants. We frequently use "wants" and "needs" as though they are interchangeable, but they most certainly are not. Understanding the difference between these two words is crucial.

The word "need" implies a necessity, something essential to well-being. In the business world, our needs are those conditions that must be met if we are going to continue to do business with a certain company. They become "conditions of sale." From this point of view, it is easy to understand that meeting customers' needs is an important investment of money, time, and energy.

Now consider "want" — a wish, a desire. Customers "want" all kinds of things: the product delivered yesterday; an immediate response to an inquiry that requires hours of search time; an order filled tomorrow that requires a week of lead time. Most of these can be negotiated. The difference, then, between a need and a want is that the latter can be negotiated, but the former cannot, because it is a condition of sale.

Wants are the "nice to haves." Needs are the "must haves." They are not add-ons. Satisfying the needs of your customer base must be integral to your product or service.

Meeting customers' needs is an investment. Wants are something you deal with when you are certain the needs are met. Customers may not be willing to pay the extra premium necessary to satisfy a want, such as more elaborate packaging or faster service.

A STATEMENT OF CUSTOMER NEEDS

All customers have a basic service need, which could be summarized as follows:

• When I deal with you, I expect that your product, your business practices, and your service will have a positive impact on me and/or my business. I expect that everyone in your company will assist me to do my job more efficiently, more productively, and more cost-effectively than your competitor.

- I assume your service intent will have a positive impact on my business.

- I expect that all my experiences with your product and your company will be good for me and my staff.

- I want you to be aware of my needs for good service. If you don't know my service needs, please ask me. I will be most pleased to review them with you.

- I would like you to be aware that my needs will change over time. Please don't try to be a mind reader. I expect you to be interested enough to talk with me from time to time.

- Please listen to me when I make suggestions to you.

This statement contains all the basic ingredients to be used to build a first class service strategy. Essentially it means that you:

- Know what the customer needs to have from your product, your service.

- Know what the customer thinks she needs as she continues to be your customer.

- Know what the customer experiences as he contacts and does business with your company.

- Correctly anticipate your customer's future needs through continuing communication with your customer.

- Have identified and clarified your own needs in the business partnership.

The high-profile, expensive aspects of your product or service are not necessarily the reason customers stay with you. When you invest the time to listen to customers and clarify their needs, you can assist them to be more effective in their own businesses. In chapter 6 you will find information on listening skills.

The basic service premise is to work with customers to

identify their needs and fulfil their expectations.

Using this statement of customers' needs in conjunction with the service statement will give staff a picture of service from both the company's and the customers' point of view.

Ensuring Customer Satisfaction: Handling Complaints

Even the best intentions to fulfil customers' needs do not always succeed. When customers are dissatisfied they have three options: say nothing and hope that things will improve; go to the competition; or complain.

Handling complaints is not the most pleasurable aspect of business, but when you consider the other two alternatives, complaints are certainly the most positive action for customers to take. Complaints are signals of customer discomfort and insecurity. A complaint is your customers' way of telling you that they want to stay with you provided you can correct the situation.

The complaint process is essential to the growth of your company. It is important, then, to listen attentively to complaints and to take action. If complaints are heard graciously and handled effectively, customers will stay with you. They will know you care, even if you cannot meet all their demands. They may even think you are wonderful for dealing with the problem so effectively. As customers, most of us will make allowances for error if we truly believe that the "guilty" person is doing everything possible to make corrections. On the other hand, an air of unconcern on the part of a business drives customers mad and sends their business away.

How do you let customers know that you've got the difficulty in hand? Talk to them, keep them informed. Let them know they are not a problem; they are your business!

It's essential for everyone in your company to know the value of complaints and to know how to respond from the first word to the final follow-up. Everyone must understand how to turn customer discomfort into customer confidence so that the customer has the satisfaction of knowing that you do care.

The two stories related below illustrate the different responses that businesses (in these cases, restaurants) can have to customer complaints and the difference a graciously handled complaint can make to a patron.

The case of

THE POACHED SALMON

Whenever my husband and I travel to the east coast, we always look forward to seafood — fresh fish superbly cooked. We dined one evening at a well-known, well-established restaurant, in the Victorian ambience of glistening silver and polished antique mahogany. Fresh poached salmon with hollandaise sauce looked like a good choice. But when it was served, we were disappointed to find the salmon dry and the hollandaise sauce browned and separated — edible but not the standard we had anticipated.

As dinner progressed, the owner came round to ask the usual question: "Was everything satisfactory?"

"Not really," we responded, "the salmon was dry and the sauce not up to what we had expected in your restaurant." Very annoyed, the owner went off to the kitchen, presumably to find out what the chef was up to.

In a few minutes, he was back, dinner plate in hand, which he then thrust at us. On the plate was a pool of hollandaise sauce, browned and crusty as before.

"The chef says the salmon was a bit dry. He doesn't know why. But the hollandaise sauce was perfectly all right. It has been under the warmer, just like this. It couldn't possibly have separated," and he pushed the plate closer for us to really see.

"Oh," we said. "Oh." We couldn't think of anything else to say! By this time, we were a source of entertainment for the other diners. The gracious dining ambience had turned decidedly chilly. We felt as though we were in some kind of combat and the final score was: one for the owner, zero for us.

It was certainly not a comfortable situation to be in, but bad experiences inevitably generate some useful service insights, so the experience had some value.

- Never ask for a customer's opinion unless you are prepared to hear the truth.

- The customer's perception of the truth may be different from yours. Be prepared to accept that.

- When you are the proprietor faced with a dissatisfied customer, it's easy to set up battle stations and win the point. Spearing the customer may be momentarily gratifying, and possibly tempting, but in the long term, it's poor business.

The Case of
THE OVER-COOKED FINNAN HADDIE

After a pleasant overnight stay in the Grand Hotel, we went down to the restaurant for breakfast, pleased to find finnan haddie, a type of smoked fish, on the menu. But sadly, when it arrived, it too was dry. When the waitress returned to ask if everything was satisfactory, we expressed our disappointment.

"I'll speak to the chef," she said.

After our last experience, we waited with considerable curiosity and some apprehension to see who would emerge from the kitchen. We imagined various possibilities: the waitress with a newly cooked breakfast? The chef with fish in hand? The manager? Or would we be taught a lesson on what we should have expected as we were in our first story? The possibilities multiplied. And, of course, we thought about what we would have done if we had been the owners of the restaurant.

A few minutes passed, then back came the waitress, looking concerned.

"The chef is terribly sorry you were disappointed, and the manager says not to charge you for the breakfast." Genuine concern showed in her voice.

With a worried look at our half-eaten breakfast, she asked, "Is there anything else we can give you? Perhaps you would like to choose something else from the menu? We don't want you to go away hungry."

Here was a staff who knew that service is about the care and nurturing of customers; about making people feel important and valued. What a contrast to our first experience!

A SERVICE MENTALITY AT WORK

At the Grand Hotel restaurant, we had seen a professional service mentality at work: care and concern for customers as the business of the organization, and staff who reflected that care and concern. In this organization, there are obviously service standards and staff who are committed to achieving those standards.

There was one other positive aspect: a customer comment card lay on the table. We decided to fill it in, to praise the service but draw attention to the quality of the meal.

We left the Grand Hotel, continued on our trip, and that particular incident was almost forgotten except as a striking contrast to our first experience. But shortly after returning home, we received a letter in response to the comment card!

DEAR MR. AND MRS. PETITE:

I would like to thank you for taking the time to write to me concerning your recent stay at Rodd's Grand Hotel.

All comment cards are reviewed by
our company president, David R.
Rodd. The suggestions and observa-
tions of our guests are valuable to us
in monitoring quality, cleanliness and
service.

I was deeply concerned to hear the
quality of finnan haddie was not up to
our standards and I will certainly
bring your comments to the attention
of the General Manager. We do appreciate your concerns, as sometimes this
is the only way we have of knowing
what is happening at the various locations.

Once again, on behalf of Mr. Rodd,
thank you for your assistance, and we
look forward to your return visit.

YOURS SINCERELY,

DOROTHY TAYLOR
DIRECTOR OF ADMINISTRATION AND DEVELOPMENT

As I read the letter, I realized I shouldn't have been
surprised that someone took the time to write. All the
indicators of a first-class service mentality were in place.

- They invited us to comment by providing the comment
  card.
- Somebody at the top (the president) reads the cards...
  and uses the information.
- They were concerned... and told us what action would
  be taken.
- They responded to our concerns... and wrote us a
  letter.

- They made us feel comfortable about the outcome of the incident.

As I read, my response was one of pleasure. I smiled and thought, "Now there's a group of people who *really* know how to run a business."

The type of service mentality predominant in any organization is quickly evident to customers. It's reflected outward by staff in each customer contact, and it either promotes or destroys customer confidence. As a business person, you need to take preventive measures to minimize the hazards of customers' discomfort.

Service is a Struggle

You build and maintain customer confidence as a result of commitment to the concept of service and daily participation in the process. This is true for staff at all levels and in any kind of business. Whether you are running a restaurant, a service station, a hospital, a school, or an industry, each person who is part of the organization must believe that service is an integral and honorable component of his or her job. However, this represents a change of attitude and practice for most people, and it can be a struggle to bring about this change. Attaining this state of mind and practice is the challenge of any service improvement program.

There are two key words here: commitment and participation. You can't have one without the other. Not only does everyone have to believe in service, they have to participate. Senior people have to lead the way, not hide in the corporate boardroom. As consultants, we are always disappointed when we are told that service is something that takes place at the junior levels. We know that any service improvement program started on that basis will have a short shelf-life and won't have much effect on long-term customer confidence.

Commitment and participation are action words. Both require a great deal of energy all of the time. To put these concepts into the daily framework of your organization requires struggle and constant vigilance. As you read on in this book, you will find that the people who have made the commitment and who participate fully have found tangible rewards in both the process and the dollar value results. You will also understand that successful approaches are not motivational programs. They are the result of carefully planned, well-orchestrated, never-ending processes. Everyone within a company participates in and has responsibilities for successful outcomes.

I certainly would not presume to tell you how to run your business, but I can tell you stories about other people and situations. I can show you what works for others and what doesn't. My experience — and that of my colleagues — tells us that although there are few absolutes, there are some aspects of service that have more impact on the bottom line than others.

You will read stories, lots of stories, about service. Why stories? Because that's what customer service is all about. Every time customers have contact with your product, your company, and your staff, there's a potential anecdote to tell. From your perspective, you want all contacts and stories to have satisfactory endings, because the total of all those experiences is the public story of you and your company.

You'll have service stories to tell as well, and I hope that as you read mine, you'll think of your own experiences and put in your own responses. In every service story, yours or mine, there's something to be learned, something we can carry away with us. We can say to ourselves, "That's just what I would have done," or "That would never go on in our company," or "I must remember to do that," or "I wonder what our customers think."

Summary

1. The quality of your service is the foundation of customer confidence.

2. Customer confidence translates into dollars worth of business. Customers will give you their business if they know that you care about their business.

3. If you ask for the customer's opinion, you must be ready for the response, even though it may be something you don't want to hear.

4. There is a critical difference between wants and needs. Customers have basic service needs. Addressing those needs is an investment in your business. Satisfying customers' wants may be a cost.

5. It's important to hear criticism graciously, to apologize for the error, and to take steps to alleviate the problem.

6. Providing excellent service is a constant struggle requiring commitment and participation at all levels. A service improvement program means a change of attitude and practice throughout the company.

Take a Break... Time Out

AS IT HAPPENED:

Overheard in an upscale shop not long ago from one salesperson to another, who appeared to be a trainee:

"Your job here is to serve the customers — and God help you if you forget that."

Perhaps that job description is a shade overstated, but the message is certainly explicit!

IN YOUR COMPANY:

- What message do you *think* your employees receive about the importance of service when they join your company, or your department?
- Who do you *think* delivers that message?
- How clear do you think the message is?
- Do your own survey. Ask some questions around the office. Now ask yourself:
  - What service message do your new employees *really* receive when they join your company or your department?
  - Who *really* delivers the message?
  - How clear *really* is the message?
  - Is there anything you would like to change about delivering the message of service to staff?

Take a Break... Time Out

AS IT HAPPENED:

A colleague of mine was fifteen minutes early for an appointment with the president of a small, profitable service company. The person behind the glass window suggested he take a seat in the waiting area until the president was ready.

But what a waiting area: three unattractive cafeteria-style chairs, out-of-date magazines, no information about the company, and a door leading directly to the outside that let in a blast of cold air each time it was opened.

The subject of the meeting was improvement of the company's customer service function and image. They wanted to develop and implement new service strategy, policy, and procedures. They believed that this might be the path to increasing their customer base and company profits.

One of my colleague's first questions was, "I suppose not many of your clients come into your offices. Most of your customer contact is over the telephone or at the client's premises?"

"Oh no," said the president, "Many of our clients come in. Why just this morning we had a group of eight."

"Well," thought my colleague, "I hope you didn't keep them waiting out there. That waiting area is not much of a place to to create an image of competency."

This company had spent thousands on the design of the logo, the company name, suitable letterhead, and advertising — all to have maximum impact on the customer. But even as the consulting process took place, the president couldn't see the need to make changes to the waiting area.

However, during the course of implementing the new service strategy, staff members suggested to the president that the waiting area could be improved: that it would be a great place to show some of the company's products, give information about the employees, and cater to the clients' comfort.

Changes were made as the staff suggested. Almost immediately, a client said to the president, "I'm certainly much happier coming in to see you now. You all seem to have a different attitude. I have the feeling everyone's taking pride in their work now."

IN YOUR COMPANY

- Who checks the reception area? Is it a place where people who have business with the company are welcomed into the offices?
- Is it a place where people can find out something about the organization and the people who work there?
- Is the receptionist welcoming?
- Does anyone care?

Take a Break... Time Out

THE BUILDING PROCESS

How can you make service a basic, daily operating principle throughout the company? Here are some suggestions.

Step one:

Identify your company philosophy, then develop a service statement that fits your particular situation (see example on page 18).

You must have a clear understanding of the implications of the statement before attempting to pass it on to others in your department or company.

Ask yourself: If I put this statement up for all to see what changes might I have to make? What would stay the same? What would be the cost/benefit to the company? Will employees see this as an advantage and why?

Step two:

Give everyone in your department/company a copy of your service statement. Ask them to think about it for the next week and share some of their thoughts with you. Tell them you think it might be a good idea to put these statements up on the wall for all to see — both staff and customers. Ask them if they have any suggestions for changes.

Step three:

At your next staff meeting, share with your staff your interpretation of the statement as it relates to the operation of the department as a whole and to particular job functions. Ask for their input. Ask what needs to be done to bring about any necessary changes in particular job functions or the operation of the department.

Step four:

Identify the service attitudes, skills, and techniques your staff need to maintain the image of service excellence.

Ask yourself: Do my staff have all the service skills they need? Do they know how to "speak" to customers under all circumstances?

Do they regard themselves as service professionals? Do they have a service mentality? Do they understand and use the language of service?

Remember: Every time customers are in contact with *anyone* in your company, they are experiencing your total package — product and service. The sum of those experiences spells either customer satisfaction and comfort — or customer dissatisfaction and discomfort. And no one stays with discomfort if there's an alternative... such as a competitor.

CHAPTER 2

THE FINE ART OF SERVICE

- ☐ UNDERSTOOD?
- ☐ ACCEPTED?
- ☐ PART OF DAILY PRACTICE?

A Talent For Service

Some people have a talent for service. These are the people who deliver the best in product, quality, and performance. They exude a "service attitude" — that is, they have a positive attitude about the importance of service, and this is reflected in their behavior toward and relations with customers.

Consider John Keyes, for example. John is manager and half the staff at a local print shop. Nothing is too much trouble for him. Customers know this, and the work piles in, often more than he needs.

The secret of John's success? He knows the fine art of service. He has a clear idea of what his customers need, what he can do, and when it can be done, and he takes the time to explain this to them. If need be, he'll suggest alternatives. If there is something extra that needs to be done for the customer, John often goes beyond the boundaries of "what I'm paid to do."

On one occasion, he noticed an error in my copy as he was setting up, and he telephoned me! "I don't read copy, as you know," he explained. "But I just noticed there was a difference in dates in two places, and I knew this was an important mailing for you, so I thought I better let you know before I went ahead. You want to fix it? But you realize this will put you a day behind in delivery because I've got to run these other jobs ahead of yours now."

John and I are truly partners: he knows my business and what I need; I know his product, including the degree of service he'll provide. This partnership approach is one of the key factors of service excellence: you and your customers working in tandem so that your product and every facet of your service lead to customer satisfaction, which will bring you repeat business and, ultimately, profit.

An example of a company with a talent for service is Paragon Industrial Photographic Reproductions Ltd. I discovered them in the Yellow Pages when I was searching for a company to do some specialized photocopying. The listing in the Yellow Pages merely reads: Paragon Industrial Photographic Reproductions Ltd. There is nothing about service in the entry, and that's too bad, because for quality of service, Paragon is one of the best.

The first time I went in, I noticed the framed letters of thanks from customers on the wall. The second time, I noticed the large words on the mat at the entrance: WE'RE GLAD YOU'RE HERE. And indeed they are. Every time you go in they make you feel welcome. Regardless of the request, Don McRobb or Paul Overend at the front desk or any one of the specialists at the back makes you feel as though you and your work really do count. Everyone there gives you the confidence that you're dealing with professionals who know that your work is important.

There are always customers at the desk, but waiting time is minimal. Paragon advertises, and delivers, speedy service. It's a growing business, with fifty employees, eighteen delivery cars, and an enviable reputation for service. They provide service over and above expectations, as the letters of thanks from customers, and my own experience, indicate.

On one occasion, I neglected to enclose my usual set of

instructions on a repeat order, but my work was on time and ready as usual. "We went ahead and did it like this because this is what you always get. Hope it's o.k. for you." And I'm one among hundreds who frequently use their services!

Another time I picked up my copies of a booklet to be used for an out-of-town seminar, but did not return to the office for another two hours. When I arrived back, there was a package from Paragon waiting for me. It contained three copies of the booklet that had been left out of the original package. I had not yet had time to miss them. "We knew you would need them" was the reply when I called to say thank you.

Like John at the print shop, the business of the people at Paragon is service. They know and care about their customers' needs. They know how to deliver. All of those letters from customers say, in one form or another, "You understood what I needed. Thanks for helping me to be successful."

Paragon's business is built on customer satisfaction — it *is* customer satisfaction. They are truly in partnership with their customers, and to many of their customers, Paragon is essential. Don, Paul, and the others have mastered the fine art of service, and that attitude translates into bottom-line results.

The fine art of service can be broken down into four essential components, as illustrated by the examples of the owners of the local print shop and Paragon.

- Having a clear idea of the boundaries of the product. Knowing what's possible and what's not. Taking the time to explain the constraints to customers.

- Taking time to understand customers' needs and expectations.

- Going that extra mile to help customers do their jobs efficiently.

- Following through!

Service: A Corporate Affair

If you are a manager or a business owner, it's tempting to think that those are a couple of nice stories but that they're only applicable to small businesses. If you have a much larger company to run, it's not easy to get everyone to think of customers all the time and to treat each as an individual. Partnership with every customer has a nice sound, but perhaps you think it's not very realistic or cost-efficient in a larger organization. Furthermore, the name of the game is profit, not teaching "the fine art of service." All employees are expected to know how to do their jobs, including service to the customer.

If these are your thoughts, you've raised two good points. First, it's definitely not easy for everyone in a company to put the customer at front and center all the time. We all have paperwork, meetings, crises, and constant deadlines. But customer satisfaction is at stake. And if customers are not satisfied, and there's a competitor just down the road, do you have an alternative?

Second, you are probably not in the business of teaching the "fine art of service." Unfortunately, very few companies are. Most of us like to believe that service skills arrive with the employee and are practiced by anyone in a service function. But minimal observation tells us this just isn't so. The reality is that modern attitudes frequently seem to be virtually anti-customer and anti-service. Service skills have been lost somewhere along the journey into the present century.

It is your job as manager to establish a professional service attitude and service mentality as a positive and essential corporate value. In North American culture, there seems to be some confusion between the words service and servitude and the behavioral implications. To many people, service seems to imply servitude, that is, a demeaning state and attitude, denoting a lack of dignity and free will. But the opposite is true. Service implies helpful acts and conduct performed with a positive attitude. Service is honorable. Service people have knowledge and expertise to aid and assist others. Their attitudes are those of professional pride.

Re-read the four critical components of the fine art of service outlined at the end of the previous section. They may be simple, but don't be deceived; they are certainly not simplistic. With planning, each one could be an integral part of every employee's job function in any organization, no matter what its size. And once you have those principles in place, you've got the beginning of a solid customer service program.

I believe there are three solid reasons for incorporating the teaching of service skills into any service improvement program, all relating to the bottom line.

1. **Staff may not know or understand basic service skills.** Service skills aren't built into educational programs. Your staff absorb skills and attitudes as they gain experience, and unless they've worked with professionals, they may have picked up some bad habits. Some of those habits could be costly in terms of customer relations. The only way to make sure your staff don't practice any bad habits is to teach them good ones.

2. **You need to attract buyers.** In many cases, customers won't buy unless they have an assured degree of service. Various aspects of service are often a condition of purchase. The quality and degree of service you are prepared to offer and guarantee become a competitive advantage.

3. **You need to maintain your existing customer base.** Continuing customer confidence is the direct result of quality service. Satisfaction means repeat business, which is the backbone of any business. Customers may talk to you about price — but it's quite possible it's quality that's keeping them: quality of product and service.

A manufacturer recently told me he stays with a certain supplier because he never has a problem with the product or people. Each order is always error-free and on time, and has been for ten years. All contact with any of the supplier's staff is always a pleasure. He could buy elsewhere at a cheaper price, but he's convinced that any other supplier would have difficulty matching that record. Think of the cost/savings benefits to both supplier and purchaser in this situation!

The guarantee of quality service initially attracts buyers, and a consistent experience of that service is what keeps them. You don't want to leave such an important component of your business to chance. Teaching your staff the necessary service skills will ensure that success of your business isn't left to chance. Teaching the fine art of service and the partnership approach is not a luxury, but rather an essential of good business practice.

Service Attitudes: The Inside Story

The fine art of customer service begins *inside* the office. The way your customers are treated often reflects the boss's attitude toward employees and, in turn, the employees, attitudes toward themselves, their jobs, and the company. Staff who feel appreciated and respected are more likely to care about customers and their concerns.

You can't teach attitudes, but you can create environments where care and concern for people in general — employees and customers — are intrinsic corporate values. We frequently hear more junior staff say, "Why don't our managers practice what they tell us to do?" Everyone on the staff of the company reflects the attitudes and behavior of the senior people. When senior people are perceived to value service attitudes and seen to practice appropriate behavior, then other people on staff will follow their examples. Staff who feel valued and who feel good about themselves and their jobs generally project good feeling, inside and outside the office, which is reflected in the quality of service they deliver.

If that sounds too simplistic, read the following two stories and judge for yourself. Put yourself in the place of the employees in both instances. Then ask yourself what your attitude is toward your own company and customers.

The case of

THE BEAMING EMPLOYEE

We were conducting a customer service program for managers. As we frequently do, we'd asked participants to identify their individual goals for the day.

One of the managers absolutely beamed. "I've just been told by one of our senior people what a good job I do and how important I am to the company. And that's why she wants me to attend this seminar. I'm here to learn everything I can. I'm needed in this company."

An interested participant? He was like a sponge in a bowl of water. He soaked up everything, as well as sharing many valuable ideas and suggestions of his own with the group. His enthusiasm and his talent for service must have been an asset to his job. He was certainly an asset during the session. Learning to serve the customer better was obviously a valued process in his company.

The case of

THE GOOD-ENOUGH EMPLOYEE

The president of a small, very busy service company was consulting with us on ways and means of improving her organization's customer service. Because there are only thirty employees, all staff talk with the customers at least some of the time.

Apparently, some customers had complained that staff frequently sounded impatient; that customers were kept on hold with no explanation; that information was often difficult to get.

During the conversation we discussed sending one

employee in particular to a seminar to improve her customer service skills, as she had been the source of several complaints. However, the president decided against this.

"She's not worth the price," she said.

"Are you going to fire her, then?" I asked.

"No. She's good enough for that job," was the reply.

What a contrast in values! It's easy to see how senior management attitudes and values set the tone and style for the way staff functioned in each of the two organizations. I wish I could say the second one was an isolated incident, but unfortunately it's not. Senior people frequently have little respect for front-line employees. Poor performance in the service area is the result.

Another illustration shows how it's often the small things that count. Front-line and support staff frequently tell me that one of their biggest problems is managers who interrupt when they are on the telephone with customers.

This is what they say:

- "Don't our managers realize those are our customers on the phone?"
- "Couldn't my boss wait until I've finished talking with the customer?"
- "Don't they respect what we are doing when we're talking with customers?"
- "I have to close my eyes when I'm on the phone with a customer so I can't see my boss waving his arms at me to get my attention. Doesn't he realize those are *our* customers I'm talking with?"

This type of distraction stops once managers realize staff need to focus full attention on any telephone conversation with customers. When it's brought to their attention, there are blushes of embarrassment and they, of course, realize the customer comes first. It's a question of re-thinking business priorities and respecting the needs of employees.

Respect and appreciation are two key components for quality service, applying equally to staff and customers. Staff who are respected and valued for their contributions will pass on that respect to customers. Adding education and training in service skills will give you a winning combination.

During one of our recent seminars, one of the participants said something like this:

> It sounds as though you are pushing me to go out there and tell my staff how much I appreciate and respect them. Listen, I pay these people. They have benefits, extra holidays. Come on now. They know they're appreciated. They get raises every year! What do you want me to do? Go out there, and tell them I love them?

Why not? A paycheck is only one form of reward. Words and actions are more immediate and often have greater impact than money. Most of us go from day to day without knowing whether or not we have any effect on the grand scheme. But most of us like to feel we're appreciated, to be told we're doing a good job when it is merited, and to be treated with respect. We like to know that what we do and how we do it really does make a difference to the organization.

At mid-morning break, during one of our seminars for front-line staff, coffee and muffins were served using good china dishes. Ruth, my associate, remarked appreciatively on this.

"Oh yes," responded one of the participants, "we're always served like this. They appreciate us here, you know."

It's probably not coincidental that at Royal Doulton there's a high standard of customer service.

The Fine Art of Service:
A Professional Attitude

As a customer, you want to know you are dealing with professionals. You want staff who know their business and understand yours. You want to be comfortable with the product and with the people behind it. When you buy a product or service, you want to feel you have a link with a responsible person should you need it.

Your customers are likely to be in contact with the designated service people on the front-line. The front-line staff are usually at the bottom of the hierarchy and have the lowest status, the least authority and often the least training and lowest self esteem. Yet it's the front-line staff who are any company's continuing link with customers. That's a sad situation and certainly not conducive to building a professional attitude.

If you are at the management level, you have authority and the status of a professional. But that's not the situation for front-line staff who frequently think of themselves as "Justas," as in, "I'm just a clerk/secretary/shipper." This is not a professional attitude but it's one often reinforced by management, as we've seen in the anecdotes and quotes earlier in the chapter.

As a customer, I feel very uncomfortable when I have to deal with a Justa. I'm never quite certain that my business will receive suitable attention. There's always a nagging doubt about whether the Justa really is a bona fide employee with authority and expertise to answer my questions and to look after my interests.

Staff who feel a strong sense of pride in their jobs and companies don't regard themselves as Justas. They know they are important to the effective operation of the business. In chapter 3, you will find some information and ideas about creating a sense of pride and professionalism among all your staff. People who are proud of their companies and their products tend to regard service excellence as the norm.

Here are the stories of two businesses that took steps to build an attitude of professionalism among the staff of the company.

A Transportation Experience

INTERAMERICAN TRANSPORT SYSTEMS INC.

Interamerican Transport Systems Inc., a company in the highly competitive transport industry, decided to tackle service improvement with a specific course of action. All of Interamerican's continuing business, continent-wide, is carried on over the telephone. That means that customer satisfaction depends not only on the efficient transportation of goods, but also on the way the customers feel they are treated when they talk to people in the company over the telephone. The way everyone communicates with customers over the telephone is crucial to the successful operation of this business.

The first step in tackling service improvement, therefore, was to have everyone, senior to junior, attend the same seminars on effective customer communication. As Mike McElhone, the president, commented, "When everyone takes the same course, we all share the same language. In our company, we work as a team. Service is our business. We want to be number one."

The second step was to develop an internal training program so that all new employees would understand the corporate values and be committed to high standards. In this company, each person knows how critical he or she is to customer satisfaction and, consequently, to the bottom line.

One of the added, perhaps unexpected, benefits of the seminars was that everyone, senior and junior, had an opportunity to hear each others' customer service concerns. At least two customer-related problems were solved during the day.

In this company, everyone is a professional. There are no Justas.

☆　☆　☆　☆　☆

A Technical Experience

BULL HN INFORMATION SYSTEMS LIMITED

Sometimes it's difficult for technical service people to deal with those of us who are technically illiterate. It's not easy to talk with your non-technical customers about a computer program that isn't working or electronic equipment that isn't functioning as it should. But, as complex technology comes into the daily lives and businesses of even the most ordinary person, technical assistance and customer service people in high tech fields are faced with the problem of talking with the people who don't understand high-tech jargon.

Bull, a world-wide information systems company, came to grips with the problem by holding customer awareness seminars for their technical assistance people. People at a variety of levels attended: managers, support staff, and receptionists, as well as the technical support staff themselves. As Jerry Webster explained to the group, "When our customers call us, they need our assistance. It's important for all of us to understand how our customers feel when they are on the receiving end. Then we're in a better position to help them."

This was a clear company message to staff: we're all in this together. Let's work on our customer communication skills. We're a team with customer satisfaction as our goal. Let's work as professionals delivering service to the customers.

This company message underlined a set of values and attitudes from senior staff. The result? An enhanced awareness and understanding of customers' needs directly affected their bottom line. Staff now saw themselves as professionals and service as an essential component of technical support.

The Fine Art of Service: Implementation

Once you've made the decision to upgrade your service to the status of excellent, where do you start? Here are some suggestions.

1. How often do your inside people get out to see customers in their offices or plants? Put yourself in their shoes. A positive professional attitude can be difficult to maintain if you never see the results or understand the importance to the customer of what you do.

    Most inside employees believe it's the boss or the sales people who go out to meet customers. They think, "We're not important enough to do that. We are just the people who...." The Justa syndrome again!

    But if customer satisfaction and service are at the heart of an operation, it makes sense to give the people directly concerned an opportunity to see the customer's business — to have an opportunity to appreciate the customer's needs.

    If you allow your inside people to go out to meet the customer and see why it's so necessary that your product arrive on time, undamaged, and defect-free, they are more likely to take the responsibility to make it happen, to feel some accountability.

    But as a manager or boss, you must tactfully do some preparation before you send people out. An informal department discussion about outside visits to customers, with participation from all, is one way of tackling difficult and sensitive issues. Not everyone automatically knows what to do in this kind of business situation. Some people may lack social and business competence. When staff represent your company they need to go out as professionals. You need to talk with them about who they'll be meeting, what questions to ask — or not to ask — and what to listen and look for. You can't assume that people with no experience of outside customer contact will have all the skills to make this a useful exercise. You may possibly, very tactfully, have to discuss what to wear, where and when to sit, when to talk, and when to listen.

You will want to reinforce the company message to the inside staff who go out to visit customers: we care about you as well as our customers. We want you to meet customers and customers to meet you. You and the job you do are important to us as well as to the customers.

Afterward, a follow-up debriefing is essential to underline the importance of customer relationships. Otherwise, visits to customers could be perceived as a way to get out of the office for a few hours, rather than as critical customer contacts. It's also quite possible you may learn some useful information. Encourage your staff to write a follow-up note of thanks to the people they visited.

2. It's not always practical for your people to go out to the customer, but a similar link and confidence can be established using photographs.

   When there's a new customer, send out a photo of the people who will be looking after his/her business, including the department manager. Introduce them as the team and encourage the customer to call them anytime and to call them by name.

   If it is appropriate, ask for a snapshot of your customer and those people in his/her business who will be calling you. Faces as well as names help your staff to feel a personal link with your customers.

   The company message to your people? Everyone here counts, both you and the customers. Here are the pictures to show it!

3. From our experience as consultants, we know there is an essential initial procedure to establishing a feeling of professionalism in a company. It sounds ridiculously simple: everyone at every level in every function uses his or her full name when answering the telephone. A full name carries authority and responsi-

bility; it sets the tone and style of professionalism. A person without a surname sounds like a Justa — and we know that Justas don't generate customer confidence.

Using a full name when you answer the telephone is the difference between unprofessional familiarity and professional friendliness. We've had people call us back, long distance from across the country, to thank us for this suggestion. (See chapter 8 for more on telephone communication and etiquette.)

4. And now, a reflective pause. As a way to enhance positive attitudes, you might like to think about finding a way to tell staff you appreciate them. It's the people in your company or department who produce results. When next you meet with your staff, is there a way you can acknowledge individual and/or collective achievements?

Summary

1. A service attitude throughout a company is essential for excellence in customer service. Taking the time to determine your customers' needs, to explain the boundaries of your product, and to go the extra mile to make sure your customers' needs are met will go a long way toward attaining customer satisfaction.

2. Staff training should be incorporated as an essential ingredient into your service improvement program. Teaching the "fine art of service" has bottom-line implications.

3. Senior people set the style and tone of a service attitude for everyone in the organization. Staff who are respected and valued by senior management will respect and value the customer.

4. Internal attitudes have a direct bearing on the quality of service directed to customers. The fine art of service

requires everyone to have a professional service attitude.

5. Creating opportunities for inside people to meet with customers helps them to identify with and appreciate customers' needs and concerns.

Take a Break... Time Out

AS IT HAPPENED:

A friend of mine sent information, as requested, to a client, then followed up with a telephone call to make certain everything was as it should be. His client, David Jones, a senior person in the company, was apparently not there. As you read the scenario, determine what your reactions would be: as my friend, as David Jones, and as a potential customer.

My friend dialed the company number.

RECEPTIONIST: AVW Company

CALLER: Dave Jones, please.

The receptionist rings through. Two rings... rings stop. Silence. Caller waits for a few seconds. Hangs up, rings back to receptionist. Explains what happened. Receptionist rings back again. Same thing happens. Two rings, then silence.

Caller listens... could be an telephone answering machine not functioning. Hangs up. Redials back to switchboard.

CALLER: I have been trying to reach Dave Jones. After two rings, there is silence, but it sounds as though the phone is attached to a telephone answering machine that isn't working properly. Do you know if he is in the office?

RECEPTIONIST: Mr. Jones is away. I will put you through to his secretary.

PERSON #1: Good morning...

CALLER: I'm trying to reach Dave Jones, but it sounds as though his telephone is attached to a telephone answering machine that isn't working properly. Are you his secretary?

PERSON #1: His secretary is away.

CALLER Well, you may be losing business because no one is answering his phone.

PERSON #1: We have just come back from holidays. I don't know anything. I'll put you through to someone who may be able to help you.

PERSON #2: Hello...

My friend explained a second time what happened when he tried to reach David Jones.

PERSON #2 (In a very disagreeable tone): Dave isn't here. I'll see if I can find someone to look at it.

Then PERSON #2 hung up and that was the end of the conversation.

After much thought, my friend wrote the following letter to David Jones, including a scenario of the telephone exchange similar to the one above.

> DEAR MR. JONES,
>
> Last Tuesday, August 5th, I called to make certain you had received the information you requested. The enclosed scenario is a result of that call. After some thought, I've decided to share it with you, since it seems to directly affect your business. I hope that you will not take offence — I think the most disturbing aspect of the whole transaction was that no one seemed to care whether or not you might be losing business.
>
> I will call you in a few days to follow up on the information I sent you.
>
> YOURS TRULY, ETC.

A few days later, my friend called Dave Jones. In the course of the conversation, he asked if his letter and scenario had been received and said he hoped that Mr. Jones did not take offence.

"Yes, I got your letter," said Mr. Jones. "We're still trying to find out who person two was." There was no further comment.

IN YOUR COMPANY:

If you were told of such an incident, what action would you take?

CHAPTER 3

SERVICE IS EVERYBODY'S BUSINESS

☐ ACCEPTED?
☐ UNDERSTOOD?
☐ BASIS FOR DAILY ACTION?

Service and the Organizational Community

Do you talk customer service or do you live it? Ask where in the organization service takes place, and you will be directed to the Customer Service person, or to the special area called the Customer Service Department, or, in large companies, to the Public Relations Department. Ask most senior executives or managers where service fits into the organizational structure and you'll probably be referred to someone at a considerably lower level who "can tell you about our service people." At any level other than the formal service level, staff will tell you they are in sales, accounting, operations, or administration. They never mention service; it's as though the greater the degree of distance from the formal service function the greater the status of their job.

There's good reason for this. Historically, service is a low status occupation. Jobs in which service is the prime function appear to have a very low rank in the organizational hierarchy. Service as a desirable way of operating business, practiced by everyone in the company, isn't the way most traditional organizations function. There's a lot of talk about service, but frequently not much action.

We must change traditional ways of thinking. Service is everybody's business, whether you are the customer service clerk or the president. Service strategies and action plans on paper are no guarantee of implementation unless there is commitment from the people who will carry them out. Every employee has to believe in the value of service relative to her/his own job. Service means action — action on the customers' behalf — and that necessitates the involvement of everyone in the organization. Service also means communicating with customers in such a manner that they know that customer satisfaction is a top priority for all staff.

Service isn't just a one-directional signal beaming outwards — one you can turn off when customers are no longer in sight. It's a value and an attitude that percolates through the entire organizational atmosphere. It is a component of everyone's daily working life, reflected in the way people work together in the organization, individually and across departments, toward a common purpose.

In an organization where service is an accepted value and basis for daily action, there is a sense of an **organizational community**, a place where people:

- Know they are there to look after customers' interests
- Understand and value the service aspect of their jobs
- Are proud to be there
- Have a clear sense and acceptance of the concept "we, the team."

Power of Synergy in Organizational Communities

The power of the "we" in the concept of community is astounding. The united action of a group of individuals produces a result or effect greater than the sum of the effects of individuals acting separately: the synergistic effect.

We all know of instances when individuals have worked together as a group and brought about enormous political, social, or economic change. This same synergy is also applicable within an organizational community.

As in any community, there's an interdependence and a network of relationships that don't show up on the organizational chart. Where an organizational community culture exists and flourishes, everyone not only values and understands this interdependence, but knows how to use relationships effectively to get the job done. People support each other, assist each other, offer service to each other. They help each other to get the job done. Managers know their prime responsibility is to assist the front-line people — the service providers — to serve the customers' needs. They know that the ultimate goal is customer satisfaction and customer confidence; that is the reason for being in business. The spirit of community is alive and well in every job function.

When the power of the spirit of community is missing, everyone — staff and customers — loses out because the "it's not my job" (I.N.M.J.) syndrome takes over and thrives like some virulent pest. The cockroach story illustrates this point.

The case of
THE COCKROACH IN THE BAR

My friend was sitting at the bar of a well-known hotel, chatting to the bartender. As he looked around, he saw two cockroaches climbing over the far end of the bar.

"There are two cockroaches over there on the bar," he pointed out.

"I know," said the bartender.

"Aren't you going to kill them?" he asked.

"Not my job," came the reply with a shrug.

My friend left his half finished drink sitting on the bar, a victim of I.N.M.J. This experience has become part of his after-dinner repertoire of service horror stories, and the name of the hotel is always included.

From a customer's point of view, do you sometimes have the feeling that whole organizations function on the I.N.M.J. premise? Do these words sound familiar?

- "It's not my job to answer her telephone if she's out."
- "It's not my job to take his messages."
- "It's not my job to see that you get your order on time..."
- "It's not my job to check the labels on those containers...

In our seminars, we use this cockroach story to show what happens when the spirit of community doesn't exist or breaks down in an organization or department. It's amazing how people identify with the story and come up with descriptions of similar incidents within their own companies. There's general agreement that the this "cockroach approach" creates a de-energizing and de-motivating work environment.

Developing the Spirit of Community

The challenge of management is to develop a spirit of community — your organizational community — if it's not already in place. Quality service is the result of teamwork on the inside: sales and production, engineering and marketing, order desk and shipping. Everyone within the organization generates and uses information; everyone is a customer of at least one other person on staff. The whole organization is a *community of customers* dependent on each other.

If the relations of the "internal customers" are negative

(if the I.N.M.J. syndrome is prevalent), then the relations of the internal customers to the external customers are also sure to be negative. On the other hand, in an organization where there is a strong sense of a "community of customers," the common goal of every member of that community is to make the team work efficiently to serve external customers effectively. Within the organization, therefore, positive working relationships are essential.

But you can't create relationships unless people understand and appreciate each other's jobs. It's surprising how little staff know about jobs in other departments, or even at other levels of their own departments. Staff are often not aware of either the total company picture or where their particular piece fits, so they don't realize how critical their information is to the next person. They may not even have a sense of *belonging* to an organizational community.

We have found that once people begin to talk with each other, explaining what they do and what's wanted, they begin to appreciate the common need for and the individual benefits of closer cooperation and more communication. There develops a feeling of understanding, responsibility, and accountability.

Senior people are frequently too involved with their own concerns to share the more global picture with staff. But Ben Harrison, president of Metropolitan Insurance, makes a point of talking with his entire staff frequently to bring them up-to-date on current changes and social trends.

> I tell my staff that we are going through a tremendous period of social change. With the technological revolution, the time for basic fundamental change is far shorter. We seem to be merging time and space. We are seeing rising consumer activism, and governments are listening. In our business, if we don't pay attention to the kinds of service the public demands, then the public will turn to alternative solutions to get it. That will be government insurance. We've got a lot at stake.

Every manager needs to believe in and build on the concept of internal customers. But first you need to find out how staff see themselves in relation to others, both their fellow workers and external customers. You don't have to run seminars or call in consultants to find this out. You might like to try this: forget the organizational chart for a few minutes and think of your department or company as a community of people working together with the common goal of customer satisfaction.

Try to put your thoughts into a picture or diagram. Sometimes people see their department or company in relation to the customer like this:

☆ ☆ ☆ ☆ ☆
the company

M
• • • • •
my department

C
the customer

Or the picture might look like this:

My department

The others in the company

☆ ☆ ☆ ☆ ☆

M

C

Or this: **M**

M   **M**

C

M   **M**

All departments surrounding your customers

As a manager, you have to decide what type of structure suits your department and company. If your art work turns out to resemble the first diagram, you may be working with a battle formation. Individuals are lined up with with no feeling of teamwork or interdependence. Community synergy will be lacking here because this is a picture of people who don't communicate effectively with, or perhaps, even look at each other.

In the second diagram, staff form a department community group, but the department manager rather than the external customer is the focal point, and the relationships with other departments, which are key to effective service, appear to be non-existent. The department is a team, but members may see the other departments as adversaries rather than part of the community. This kind of picture indicates the need for relationship building. Encourage members of your department to see themselves as an essential part of the community network and to identify what they can reasonably expect from each other. Conflicting needs are inevitable, but when people learn to respect each other, compromises can be worked out. Use the power of synergy to get things done.

The last diagram emphasizes the importance of both the internal relationships and the external customer. By grouping the various departments around external customers, you show how individuals and departments function collectively, using the synergy of the organizational community, to work toward that ultimate goal — customer satisfaction. You could overlap the circles to show the degree of interdependence between departments as well as the effect of this interdependence on customers.

If your pictures look more like the first two diagrams, you need to change the picture. You need to encourage people to see themselves as belonging to an organizational community.

We have identified two factors that are key to developing an organizational community.

1. The manager's job is to create a sense of community by encouraging staff to find out about each other's jobs

and to help each other. Most people know little about the day-to-day activities of others, and they inevitably find this type of information interesting. This exchange promotes a much greater degree of mutual understanding and cooperation.

One very effective approach is to arrange a series of lunch time gatherings for people from various departments to give short presentations about their jobs — what they do, how they do it, and who they depend on for information. This type of exercise encourages people to give serious thought to their own jobs in relation to others, particularly those in other departments. They have a better understanding of how they fit into the larger picture, and why the needs of others deserve to be respected.

Of course, not everyone feels comfortable about or is skilled at doing this kind of presentation. But even this can be used to advantage — staff can ask each other for help and suggestions. There are also courses, video tapes, and books available as resources. You can encourage the use of visual material and make the equipment available. You never know — out of all this may come some useful ideas for client presentations.

Most important, you will be pleased to find how much goodwill is generated when people begin to understand and appreciate each other's jobs. This is a good foundation for community spirit and the beginnings of a cooperative attitude.

2. Managers must build a sense of pride in the organizational community. You need to recognize the individual efforts of your employees. You need to create champions. Staff need to feel that they count as individuals and have some importance in the overall plan. If you are in a senior position or in one of the higher profile jobs such as sales where you can see the results of your labors, you know when you are a star. But it's often difficult for others to get a sense of any excitement or importance about their jobs. Unless someone makes a point of telling them otherwise, some staff

may think of themselves as just part of the day-to-day routine with no particular individual importance in the company — a Justa.

When individual contributions are recognized, staff feel a greater sense of pride in their jobs and in belonging to the organizational community. Think up ways that you can give credit when it's merited, and make champions of your staff members.

CREATING A CHAMPION

We conducted a seminar for some of the employees of United Cooperatives of Ontario, a rural retail chain that has a radically changing customer base. Their customers are no longer just the local farm and rural community, but weekenders from the city who have bought recreational farms. That's a new challenge for the staff who now have to know how to look after both types of customers: professional farmers who know exactly what they want and part-time novice farmers who need more guidance and advice.

During the seminar, Lloyd Crawford, the area manager, asked us if we'd mind if he took just a few minutes at the end of the day. He didn't tell us why, so we had no idea what to expect. Just before wrap-up time, he took over the floor and, with a great sense of consequence and gravity, said he had a communication of great importance. He then read out a letter received from one of those part-time novice farmers, congratulating the area manager on the operation of one of his stores and on the helpfulness of one staff in particular, whom he named in the letter. The manager then presented a copy of the letter to the salesperson to great applause from everyone.

Now that's creating a champion!

Service Language: Striving for a Common Understanding

In some of our seminars, we do a simple exercise with Lego to show how, given the same tools to work with, people produce different results. Everyone gets the same number and shape of Lego pieces, and we ask people to put them together very quickly. Very seldom are the final results similar to one another. One participant asked, "How can we all make such different things with the same pieces?" "Easy," we replied. "Although we all start out with the same pieces, or use the same words and phrases, each of us frequently has a different understanding of the pieces or words we use."

But a lack of common understanding presents problems. When you function as a team, as part of a community working towards a common goal, everyone needs to have a mutual understanding of the words used. It sounds elementary and simple, but in practice it's not always easy.

Take the phrase "customer service," for example. In our workshops, we've learned that not everyone thinks of customers or service in the same way. Ask your staff, "Who are your customers? Tell me about them." There will be a variety of responses.

- "The people/companies who buy our products."
- "We don't have many customers. We deal mostly with our distributors/wholesalers."
- "I don't know our customers. I work/deal only with other departments."
- "People on the other end of the telephone who complain."
- "I'll refer that question to our sales manager."
- "Our department doesn't have customers. We look after administration services."

This diversity of responses reveals some rather narrow interpretations. When you consider that customer service begins inside the company, these responses have some dangerous and definite implications.

Staff usually think of customers as depersonalized units such as market segments, numbers and frequency of orders, monthly billings, or credit ratings. They may even consider customers as interruptions to the really important work, such as solving a technical problem, meeting a deadline for the month-end report, or balancing the cash for the day. Most employees rarely think of their co-workers inside the company as customers with similar service requirements. And staff who are not directly in contact with external customers often have difficulty relating their jobs to customers and to customer satisfaction. If you have had the experience of waiting to pay at a service desk while the clerk counts the cash for the bank deposit, you will know what I mean. That clerk does not equate "customer" with "priority."

Think of your own circumstances. You are working on something you need to finish before the end of the day. Pressure is building. The telephone rings. There's a customer on the other end with a seemingly trivial question. At times like that, it's not always easy to remember that without customers you wouldn't be in business!

When we ask people in our seminars to explain what they mean by the term "service," we fill up several sheets of flip-chart paper. Our experience shows that we simply cannot assume that the word service means the same thing to any two people — at any level in any organization or business. The true story below illustrates this point.

The Case of
THE RAISINS IN THE MUFFINS

My friend decided to use the half hour between two appointments to relax with a cup of coffee. He went into a local café, sat down at the counter, and ordered the coffee. He was the only person there, so the waitress had time to chat with him. Pleasantly, she asked if he'd like one of the fresh muffins as well.

"Providing there are no raisins," my friend said.

"I don't know about the raisins, but here's what I'll do. I'll cut the muffin in half, and if there are any raisins, I'll cut them out. O.K.?"

My friend agreed, and as it turned out that there were raisins, she began removing them with a knife. But just as she was well into the raisin extraction, the boss came in.

"What the hell do you think you're doing?" he shouted at the top of his voice.

"Picking out the raisins for this gentleman."

"I don't pay you to pick out raisins." He grabbed the plate and slammed it down in front of my friend. "There is your muffin."

"Fine, but I won't pay for it if there are raisins in it," said my friend.

There were raisins and my friend didn't pay. And he didn't go back.

☆　☆　☆　☆　☆

If you and your staff don't have the same understanding of service, or service standards, the customer's requirements get lost. You need to ask your employees what service means to them, and then listen to make certain that everyone agrees on the definition and on the ways to put it into practice.

A manager we know developed the following exercise for his department meeting. He gave every staff person an envelope containing the following words, typed and enlarged, each on a separate slip of paper.

PEOPLE	YOURS	OUR
PERSON	ACKNOWLEDGE	COMMUNICATE
NEED	IMPORTANT	BUSINESS
WANT	HELP	NEED(S)
ACTION	PRIORITY	COMMUNICATION
YOU	CARE	PARTNERSHIP

He asked them to think of "service" then to pick five words in order of priority that fitted with their idea of service and explain the choice to the group. If they wanted to use other words, they could.

At the beginning of the discussion, "action" had top priority. "Everyone knows service is what you do," one participant said. "You get the product out to customers. You make sure it gets there on time, in good condition. You answer questions."

But as they talked, "communication" and "communicate" took on more and more importance. They discovered that effective communication is the basis of their service. Information flow in the right directions, at the right time, both internally and externally, is critical to quality service. This conclusion led to some soul-searching about their methods of communication, including monthly statements, billings, order desk, and handling of complaints. The outcome was a decision to take a long, hard look at some specific areas within the company.

In this case, exploring the word "service" brought out individual ideas, and then guided the group to a mutual understanding and acceptance of the concept of service for that particular department. No risk of another version of the raisin story here.

The young manager who used this exercise has learned early that clear communication is the basis of understanding. Realizing that people may talk about service without thinking of what the term actually means to them in terms of daily action, he created an opportunity to clarify ideas and identify priorities.

Remember: You can never assume that you and your staff mean the same thing even though you are using similar words. When you are dealing with something as critical to the bottom line as customer satisfaction and customer confidence, taking the time to make certain everyone shares a common understanding is an investment in success.

Service Professionals

As an employer or manager, you need to create an atmosphere of professionalism throughout your organizational community. You need to oust the Justa syndrome.

Customer service and customer satisfaction begin inside the organization. The way your people feel about themselves, the way they see their jobs, the way they are regarded and rewarded by bosses and colleagues all directly influence their attitudes toward customer service. All of these factors help to create the picture of the service person as either a professional or a Justa.

Let's identify the characteristics of the service professional from both employees' and employers' perspectives.

The employee who is a service professional:

- Is found at any level of the organization
- Is valued by his/her employer and knows this
- Respects his/her job
- Appreciates the jobs of others
- Learns, understands, and uses service skills
- Makes customers feel valued and respected
- **Delivers quality service performance**

The boss who is a service professional:

- Knows that management sets the tone and style for everyone in the organization
- Values his/her people and tells them so
- Respects the front-line service jobs and the people who do them
- Takes the time to learn what people do in their jobs
- Provides continual opportunities for staff members to learn service skills
- Shows all staff that he/she values and respects customers

- **Delivers quality service performance**
- **Sets an example for others**

Read over the "Case of the Beaming Employee" and the "Case of the Good-enough Employee" in chapter 2, applying these characteristics where appropriate. It's easy to pick out the service professional.

A Service Mentality and Language

Every organization has a definite mentality as part of its corporate culture. Whether or not a service mentality is the norm depends on the direction given by senior management. Most of us have experienced the kind arrogance that leaves you wondering if customers are part of the business plan. As customers, we tend to accept that kind of experience only once before we go off to the competitor.

The language used by staff not only reflects the company service attitude and mentality, it also promotes definite responses from customers. Language is a powerful service tool. The language you use can keep customers coming back or drive them away.

Like any tool, your service language needs to be kept in good condition, taken out to be examined for wear and tear, and given regular maintenance. This language is a mirror of your service attitude, philosophy, and day-to-day operations. It tells customers how much you value their comfort level as buyers and as people.

Service language gives the message, "I am here to serve your interests," not "I'm just a clerk/junior/secretary so I can't help you" (the Justa Syndrome).

Service language is a language of pride and *professionalism*. Service language tells customers that you have the knowledge, the experience, the expertise, and the resources to assist someone who needs: direction, information, an error corrected, a problem solved, or a product ordered. It's the language of a person who is in control of the situation — a service professional.

A service mentality is based on the critical premise that everyone in the company is a service professional and knows and uses service language. The first holiday dining story in chapter 1 illustrated a lack of service mentality and a lack of understanding of service language. Even proprietors need to review their service language skills!

Remember: Service attitudes, skills, and techniques are essential components of good business practices. It's essential to provide opportunities for staff to learn them.

Summary

1. A critical element of quality service is the understanding that service is a value, endorsed by all staff as a desirable way of operating business, practiced by everyone in the company, at all levels.

2. People working together within an organization constitute an organizational community. Within this community, staff are customers of each other, generating and using resources and information. If people treat each other as customers, the I.N.M.J. ("it's not my job") syndrome is unlikely to surface.

3. You can build the spirit of community by encouraging people to become familiar with and respect each other's jobs, by fostering a sense of belonging, and by creating opportunities for champions to be recognized.

4. Everyone within the organization must have a common understanding of the words "customer service" as these relate to their jobs.

5. Staff must think of themselves as professionals. A service mentality and language based on professionalism lead to customer confidence and satisfaction.

Take a Break... Time Out

AS IT HAPPENED:
A colleague of mine was asked by a client to attend a meeting with senior executives to discuss a new customer service training program to be developed for a rapidly expanding chain of retail stores. The timing wasn't convenient for my colleague, but he agreed to attend because the senior people judged it to be a matter of high priority and great urgency. He arrived promptly at the designated time, and was asked to please take a seat because the people concerned were in a meeting. So he sat down to wait... and wait.

Although the reception area was pleasant, there was no information about the company or reading material of any kind. Off to one side, two employees were engaged in a lively discussion about their personal lives. As the minutes went by, my colleague became increasingly edgy. After all, he had come at the request of a senior executive. At the end of fifteen minutes, he asked the receptionist to please find out how much longer the present meeting might be. After an inquiry the receptionist assured him it would be "just a few minutes."

"What do you mean by just a few minutes?," he asked.

"Oh, five or maybe ten," she said.

Twenty minutes later, he had had enough. He was just about to leave his card and a note with the receptionist and take his leave, when one of the executives came out and, without even a perfunctory apology, announced, "We're ready to start the meeting now."

IN YOUR COMPANY:
This was certainly not an incident with catastrophic consequences in any of the participants' lives, but as I listened to my colleague tell his story, it seemed to me to be a significant event that could have negative consequences through the company.

I asked my colleague if he believed that this event indicated an attitude, manner, and style at the senior level of this company that might have a spill-over effect on customer service as provided by staff.

How would you have responded?

Where does customer service begin and end? Is customer service something you expect your employees to do while senior people get on with the "real" business of running the company?

CHAPTER 4

MANAGEMENT
A Bellwether for Excellence

❐ ACCEPTED?
❐ UNDERSTOOD?
❐ PART OF DAILY PRACTICE?

Management as Bellwethers

A bellwether is a person who takes the lead or sets the trend in a group of people. In the last chapter, we looked at an organization as a strong community of internal customers. Communities need leaders, people who provide vision, direction, goals, expectations, care, and nurturing. In the organizational community, it is senior management who provides this leadership. They are the bellwethers for the rest of the company; they are the organizational community leaders and role models.

Where senior people lead, staff members will follow. The attitudes managers have about the company's product and service, the ways they deal with customers, both external and internal, will be the standard by which staff set their own attitudes and actions and those of their subordinates. These are the standards that will appear in the finished product or service. The signals that come from the top clearly state one of two messages:

"Good Enough Is Good Enough For Us"

OR

"Excellence Is Our Goal."

Before you choose which of the two messages you want to send out to your company and customers, read the following story.

The Case of

THE SHAKY STANDARDS

The XYZ printing company was operating a successful business. They had a number of long-term, key account customers who provided a substantial financial base. Defective orders were a problem, but not to the point where they were losing customers. Their service, and presumably their prices, accommodated appropriate corrective action.

However, with the rapid proliferation of printing companies, the XYZ company found itself in an extremely competitive position. A very large order was found to be defective by a major account and was returned with instructions to remedy the situation or to face losing their business. This coincided with other, somewhat less costly concerns. The company was still profitable, but faced with the potential loss of a large chunk of revenue, senior management decided the time had come for some definitive action.

Consultants were called in for advice. There were indeed problems — morale problems, compensation problems, and management problems — all contributing to lack of quality standards and accountability to customers.

After preliminary discussions, the consultants proposed a plan of action with emphasis on quality and service. After two weeks of thought, the president turned down the proposal with these words: "I've done a review of our competition and I find that we are no worse than others in our business. We've decided not to go ahead at this time."

Before you make your judgement about this incident, consider the situation. The basis of business is profit. This company was still in a profit position. If the president was correct in his assessment of their market position with respect to the competition, why change? Change involves commitment of time, energy, and finances. He was not prepared to make a commitment of time and resources for a goal that seemed to be unnecessary.

Here is the dilemma. If the competition is no better, and perhaps even somewhat less competent, then why strive for a higher standard, for improved quality and service? Will improving the quality of your total service package improve your bottom-line figures? Perhaps not immediately. But consider the resources you have to commit to poor quality. The cost of re-doing a defective order, the cost of customer dissatisfaction, and the cost of losing an account to a competitor all have significant dollar implications. Can you afford those costs?

Change, of course, also involves costs. Resources and energy are required. Perhaps the standards in that particular business were satisfactory as measured against others. Any customers assessing the competition might find things were no better. They might decide that changing suppliers would be an added cost that, in the long term, would have no measurable benefits. But that is a considerable risk to take over the long term.

Here are some further details about the management of the XYZ printing company. The president's expectations of staff were never explicitly stated. He believed that staff ought to know what was expected of them in their jobs without being told. He had never made clear to anyone in the company, at any level, his expected standards of performance as daily operating policies except as a reaction to an event. His response to crises that occurred was, "You ought to have known better."

He believed in specific rewards for not making mistakes rather than in generally encouraging people toward excellent performance. Bonus systems were in place based on errors. If you made mistakes, dollars came off your bonus. Consequently, most people were more interested in hiding errors than in achieving top quality. Complaints had a way of disappearing into desk drawers. As a result, minor situations frequently escalated to major crises.

This is certainly not the description of a dynamic, forward-looking organizational community. Since their standards were based on the poor performance of the competitors, if the competition made one move forward toward improvement of service and quality, this company would be in trouble.

In this instance, staff modeled their performance on the management style coming from the top: reaction, concealment, and punishment, rather than action, openness, and encouragement.

Management Standards

Which standards are you going to choose to be a role model for your company? Here are four key questions to ask yourself that will help you clarify your thinking.

1. What do I mean by quality and excellence as these pertain to my product, my customers, my staff, the way I run my business, and my bottom line?

2. If I choose the "good enough" standard today, what impact will that decision have on my product, my customers, my staff, and my bottom line in the future?

3. What is my personal philosophy and set of values for doing business? Do I believe that customer satisfaction is the result of good internal customer relationships? Do I believe that senior people are the role models for staff? Do I believe that my people will take responsibility for providing top quality work if I lead the way?

4. Am I making a short-term decision or looking at future considerations in relation to my market niche?

You can see that these questions emphasize the importance of taking the future into consideration. I asked Ben Harrison, president of Metropolitan Insurance, if he thought that service excellence translated into *future* bottom-line results:

> Absolutely. Tremendous pressures exist within all companies today. By making our customers enjoy doing business with us, we will have people beating a path to our door. When times get tough, as they are right now, we have to deal with our brokers on a pretty hard-line basis because we want a certain quality of business. But if they enjoy doing business with us because we have a solid foundation of excellence as a constant, not something that swings up and down, this will transcend a tremendous number of problems that we must have in a cyclical business. It all helps to bridge the gap, even in difficult times.

Here is a way of looking at service excellence, not just taking into consideration your bottom-line results of today, but looking at your business as a partnership with the customer that you need to build and maintain for the future.

Of course, you know your own business best. Only you can answer these fundamental questions. The service standards you set will depend on your responses. Obviously we hope that you have opted for the standard of excellence.

THE STUFF OF EXCELLENCE

Excellence is the stuff of business. It is recognizable and dynamic. You know when you've experienced it. It sparkles:

> Excellence is an international currency that sparkles with confidence. People

who are champions of an idea, people
who get things done with a single-
minded yet versatile sense of accom-
plishment, can generate sparks. You all
recognize that sparkle.

DR. GERALDINE KENNEY-WALLACE
SCIENCE COUNCIL OF CANADA

Excellence as international currency? Yes! As trade
barriers come down, excellence may be your single most
profitable competitive advantage. When your standards
are high and your people take pride in working to those
high standards, you have an enviable situation and product. Excellence has impact, on both people and markets.

Excellence is organic and pervasive. You can sense the
presence of excellence within minutes of walking into an
organization. There is a specific ambience, a glow, that
goes with excellence that has nothing to do with the cost
or extent of the interior decorating.

When excellence as the standard of achievement is the
norm, you can sense that it is present in every corner of an
organization. Excellence constantly beckons everyone in
the organizational community toward the best.

People who subscribe to the standards of excellence
know it is not something you put on paper today and shove
in a desk drawer until you have time to get it out again.
They know and accept that this is the way of life in their
organizational community. They work in an environment
where managers provide the role model for community
cooperation and excellence.

The Courage To Generate Sparks

Managers must have the courage to be role models for
excellence. In any group, people emulate dominant behavior. That's why role modeling is such a powerful psycho-
logical and behavioral tool. It can be used in either a

negative or a positive way. In the "Take a Break" section at the end of this chapter, an interview with Ray Hould, executive vice president of All-Way Transportation, focuses on the power of the positive approach.

Positive role modeling is the best way to actively promote the growth of an individual or company-wide service mentality. It's the best and also the cheapest teaching device yet invented. When staff see and hear everyone at the senior level not only talking but also living excellence and service, they know that service excellence is the expected norm.

But it's not enough to tell staff what to do, or to provide training courses. Staff must see top-level people practising what they preach. As consultants and trainers, one of our most frustrating experiences occurs when staff say to us, "If this is what they want us to do, why don't you tell the people at the top they should pay attention to these things as well?"

Leadership means you are encouraging people to follow you as you show them the way. "Pushing" — telling people what they ought to be doing — doesn't work.

The Power of Signals

The power of role modeling stems from the fact that actions speak louder than words. Your actions send messages to staff about what is and isn't an acceptable attitude or practice. These signals, then, are very powerful tests for implementing a certain expectation of the day-to-day practices of staff.

You must become conscious of the signals that your actions impart. Think of the messages the following convey.

- Meetings that always start late.

- An "Open Door" policy but a secretary who screens people who want to see you.

- Lack of interest in the staff at the lower levels.

- Little or no communication with staff who actually perform the traditional service functions.

PRECEPTS FOR SIGNALING EXCELLENCE

Four key precepts guide the day-to-day activities of managers who achieve service excellence. These managers are aware that role modeling is a powerful tool for signaling the message that "Excellence is Our Goal."

1. **Practice what you preach.** Not only what you say but what you do signals your expectations. If you preach it, practice it. If you expect things to be done on time for external customers, make sure you get things done on time for your customers inside.

   If you say something is so in your company or department, such as "My door is always open. I want to hear from you any time," make certain staff see and experience what you've said. If it isn't realistic, don't try to do it, and certainly don't promise it.

   You want your staff to keep the promises they make to customers. You want that kind of honesty and commitment to be one of the working principles of your company. You must, therefore, let staff see that you also adhere to these principles yourself; you are the symbol for day-to-day company expectations.

2. **Be explicit.** Never assume that your staff know what you have in your mind. Unless you have shared your values and performance expectations, your staff are working on assumptions that could be faulty. As you saw in the "Case of the Shaky Standards," this is not a solid base from which to operate.

   In order to be explicit to others you have to be explicit to yourself first. What are your values? What are your expectations of yourself? It's surprising how much difficulty most of us have when we have to be specific about intangibles such as values. We think we know exactly what we would say until the time comes to make a public statement. That is why it is essential to take the time to articulate your values to yourself before going public.

Expectations have to be stated as tangible results that can be measured. To say to staff that you expect them to deliver quality product and excellent service is not enough. You have to spell out what this means in a concrete way:

- Products checked for defects before being sent to customers.

- Letters checked for errors before they are signed.

- Callers greeted courteously over the telephone.

Each of the above is an example of an activity that can be measured as either up to your standards or not.

The ability to be clear and specific is a distinct signal to staff that someone is interested and cares.

3. **Be consistent.** For this, you need to have sorted out and articulated your values. You want staff to know that you always demand the same quality of performance. You want them to know that as far as you are concerned, service is not on a pendulum. When you are consistent, your staff does not receive mixed signals about what is acceptable. The goal is clear in everyone's mind.

4. **Listen.** You cannot have excellence of product or service unless you know how to listen to your staff members. When you listen, you know what is going on: you know what needs to be changed and what needs to be maintained in order to keep up the standard of excellence.

When you are listening you are signaling your interest and your desire to understand and respond. You are saying to your staff member, "I want to hear what you have to say. I am taking you seriously." This is particularly important with front-line people. They are the slim point on which your success is poised because they deal with your product and your customers all day. They are also the people with the ideas for improvement. In addition, if you signal your readiness to listen to your internal customers, they will get the message that listening is a valued trait, and they will be more willing to listen to customers.

Every organizational community has its own symbols that signal communication patterns. Some signal closed doors; some say, "Let's talk. I'll listen." Ben Harrison explains the situation at Metropolitan Insurance:

> In this company, management is very approachable. We are open to listening and we try to respond. We introduced "bitch boxes," brass mailboxes set up in several areas of the office for suggestions and complaints. All of the notes come directly to me. Everybody gets an answer. If they identify themselves, they get a personal written reply from me. These are not shared with other managers unless I have permission. If there's no identification, then I give a general response in the monthly meeting.

At All-Way Transportation, managers' offices are in easily accessible locations and staff are encouraged to stop in. Ray Hould has an interesting point of view of management responsibility: making the jobs of the front-line people easier, by listening to front-line staff while they tell him how they can be more efficient and effective.

Signs and Symbols

Earlier in the chapter, I mentioned that you can sense excellence, or the lack of it, when you walk into an organization. Unconsciously you react to the ambience, the environment. Most people are not conscious of the signs and symbols that mold their perceptions of the environment. But it's from these perceptions that you build up a set of expectations of how things will be. Signs and symbols are therefore very important. As a manager, you have to become conscious of the signs and symbols that exist in your working environment. You have to make sure the right ones are in place and the wrong ones weeded out.

SIGNS AND SYMBOLS: NEGATIVE AND POSITIVE MESSAGES

First there are the negative signs and symbols:

- On the head secretary's desk in the front office of a school: "You would have to be crazy to work here." Is this supposed to inspire students?

- Sign at the entrance of a public agency. "All visitors report to the front office." But inside, no indication is given of the location of the front office.

- A large sign says "Service Desk" on the department store floor. The reality is that service is not part of the operation — the sign should read "Cash Desk."

- The "reception" area of a company completely lacking in information about the company, or any reading material of any kind. The term "reception" in these circumstances is a false representation of the facts.

Then there are the positive signs and symbols:

- The "reception" area with attractively presented and interesting information about the organization including the company mission statement and service pledge proudly displayed.

- A large and flattering picture of the employee of the month, with relevant information, posted on a company bulletin for all staff to see.

- A new company product displayed in a manner that encourages all staff to read the pertinent information and become familiar with the product.

The presence of positive signs and symbols is an indication of an environment in which everyone, as a matter of course, will do their best. When you are considering a service improvement program, you need to think about the symbols in your environment and the messages they send to staff.

Summary

1. As senior management leads, company people follow. The messages that come from the top signal either "Excellence" or "Good enough." Managers are the role models for their staff.

2. Managers need to identify and set standards for quality service. The decisions you make now will affect your future bottom-line results.

3. Four key precepts guide the day-to-day activities of managers who achieve service excellence: signal excellence — practice what you preach; be explicit; be consistent; listen to your staff.

4. Staff have to know what the standards are so they know what they are striving toward. As a manager, you develop signs and symbols that create an environment for service excellence.

Take a Break... Time Out

AN INTERVIEW WITH RAY HOULD
All-Way Transportation Corporation is a school bus transportation company. The present senior executives, Rick McGraw and Ray Hould, took over the company in 1983 and in five years have made it tops in the field. When I first worked with people in All-Way, I was impressed with the desire for excellence that I found throughout the company,

as well as the staff dedication to service. They have a true organizational community spirit, which pays off in an enviable reputation for excellence.

I spent a morning with Ray Hould, executive vice president, and he talked about his organization.

ANNE PETITE: My impression of All-Way is that of an organization in which everyone is committed to service, in which the service attitude prevails throughout. That doesn't happen by accident. As a senior person, would you tell us what you've done to influence and promote this service attitude?

RAY HOULD: When I'm asked this question, one term flashes through my mind, the one we use as our philosophy: people come first. There are lots of business requirements, procedures, policies, and reports to write, but we've always attempted to put people first. For example, we have an open-door policy. In many companies, you can never get by the secretary. But we have always strategically located our management people close to the entrance doors of our various buildings. We're more visible. There's more of a tendency for people to walk in. We put people ahead of everything else.

A.P.: It must be very difficult to maintain that contact when you have so many diverse groups of employees. For example, you have hundreds of part-time bus drivers.

R.H.: That was a real concern when we took over the company: how we could maintain contact with all those people who only come in to the office once every two weeks. So we created situations where there has to be contact. For example, every second pay day, we clear out our maintenance garage, clean the floors with solvent, and cover the work benches. That morning, the mechanics don't work. We have a catering service come in to serve croissants, and Danishes. They use china cups, stainless steel cutlery, and butter in dishes. As well as the part-time drivers, the managers, staff, and mechanics attend, and everyone wears name tags. Everyone is part of the team.

A.P.: Management leading the way for a team approach?

R.H.: Yes. A team is much stronger than individuals. While it takes leadership, it also takes commitment from everybody to follow that leadership. You have to have the passion to win, to be part of that team.

A.P.: I'm interested to hear you use that word passion. Tom Peters (*In Search of Excellence*) talks about the passion for doing things right the first time, and that's what I hear from you.

R.H.: Yes. And you will get that from any of our managers. As a matter of fact, I think you will get that from anyone in our organization. They each have a passion for doing their jobs to the best of their ability.

A.P.: How do you get the commitment to "best?"

R.H.: You take the time to ensure that when you are talking to people you devote yourself to listening and responding. People come first. People are our business. Therefore we treat our employees with respect, give them priority. We have a family-style business.

I believe the family that plays together, stays together. That's true in business as well. We have many social functions through the year — a Christmas party, golf tournaments, safe driving awards, and driving championships — to promote the family spirit. You can't just drive your bus or sit at a desk and get your pay check, because after a while it becomes dull routine. You have to inject some passion into it. Everything has to be done with a passion so that people come first, because it's the people who make it happen. None of us has a job if they don't do their job right.

And you can't forget to tell them. We all remember what it was like when we were down at the grass roots level doing the missionary work. Too many of us, when we get up to senior management, forget what it was like: how isolated you could feel; how you didn't really know who your boss was or who the senior man was. You might have seen his picture in the corporate magazine. He never came over and put his arm around you and said you were doing a good job. But we encourage that.

A.P.: When you hire a new manager, how do you find someone who will fit in with your philosophy of doing business?

R.H.: We go through the selection process very carefully. Once we've narrowed the selection to one or two people, they'll be interviewed by the manager, then by me, and then by the people who would make up their peer group.

When I see them I am informal and casual. I talk about corporate history, philosophy. I get them to talk about themselves, their personal beliefs and philosophies. What they did in their last job is not relevant in this interview. Every organization has its own culture, and we want to know how this individual will adapt to this culture. You create a new mix every time you bring in a new person.

Then there's the meeting with the peer group. This could last one hour or four. We rely on their input, often more than logic dictates. The kind of people who get the job have come to grips with their own egos. Too many senior managers get wrapped up in their own self importance. We want people who will interact with the employees — go up to them and say "Hi"; ask, "Any problems with the system?" "Parents giving you a hard time?" Say "How are you?" and mean it. You've got to listen and pay attention, be prepared to interact. It doesn't take a lot.

Right from day one, R.M. and I interacted with the people. When we first acquired the company, we had to get to know the business. We shared an office next to the dispatch center. It was the best place for us to be in terms of our commitment to doing a good job and to operating a family-style business. We talked with the people who would have to change first, the drivers. They came in and told us about the business. It was their ideas that we were going to implement.

In 1984 we got into trouble because of a number of

circumstances and we could have lost a major contract. But we went to the driver group. I remember the day I stood up in front of forty or fifty drivers and told them, "We're in trouble. We need your help to provide the service we know we have to provide." And without exception, they volunteered: "What do you want us to do?"

We had to depend on those drivers. They would work all night proofing and matching the lists of school boards, children, and routes. Then they would leave to do their runs, go home to get some sleep, then come back the next night.

They never mentioned money, but of course we kept track of their hours. When it was all over, we paid them. I know of several drivers who didn't expect to be paid. One woman in particular came to me and asked why we'd given her this check. "I didn't expect to be paid for this. We were in trouble. We had to save the company." She didn't say "you," she said "we."

We have a driver who had been working for twenty years for the company. When we took over in 1983 there were only a couple of hundred people driving for us, so we got to know them all by name. At the first few social functions, I noticed that she was missing, so I asked her why she didn't come. She always had a reason. She finally showed up at a Christmas party in 1986. I saw her come in. I pinned a corsage on her. Later I went over and told her, "I'm glad to see you here. I'm really glad you could come." She said, "Well, I've heard so much about these parties, I just had to come and see for myself." Then she said, "You know, I've got to tell you something. All the years I worked with the company, I never let anyone know where I was working. As a matter of fact, I always parked my bus two blocks away from the house, so no one would know where I worked. But since you people took over, I'm proud of where I work. I park my bus in my driveway, right in front of my house, because I want everyone to know I work for All-Way."

That was very gratifying, because she was one of the old group, hard core, who believed that things would never get any better. And there she was, waving the flag, with the kind of passion that is so important. She's got the passion, the commitment. She's part of the team.

A.P.: What gave her the passion?

R.H.: The fact that from the first time she expressed dissatisfaction with what we were doing, we took the time to say, "Come in, sit down, let's talk. We want to see you."

A.P.: She is part of the quality service you provide. I'm impressed with the degree of responsibility all your people assume — your customer information operators, for example.

R.H.: Those are difficult jobs to fill. The only time people phone is to talk about a problem. The jobs needed to be restructured to reduce the stress. We tried longer breaks first, but that didn't work, so now they work four days a week. We talk with them, recognize what they are doing. They know we care, so they care too. They have a sense of proprietorship about their jobs and the company. They deal with the problems with passion and caring. And they are given the authority to take action. They get recognized for taking the initiative for solving the problem.

A.P.: You've talked about passion again! Is that what makes your service a quality service?

R.H.: It's not so much what you do as how you do it. To be successful, you've not only got to react, you've got to be proactive about potential problems, to be responsible for your own destiny — you've got to have passion.

We've become leaders in the field. I'm very proud of the success we enjoy today. But it isn't just me, it's everyone behind me doing the best that they can do.

Take a Break... Time Out

CREATING A SERVICE PROFESSIONAL

I visited a prospective client, the president of a small, very successful manufacturing company.

"Come in to my office," he said, "I would like you to meet Susan Smith. She's a new sales person here. Susan is new to this business, so she is going to spend the next two weeks here in my office with me, listening to what goes on in this company. At the end of two weeks, she'll know what this business is all about, and she'll know how I handle customers."

Amazing! How many people in your company would be willing to have someone listen in to every aspect of their jobs, including handling difficult people — customers both inside and outside the company?

SOME QUESTIONS TO CONSIDER:

Do you believe that it is the manager's responsibility to seize every opportunity to teach people to do their jobs? Is the manager's role that of educator?

What do the signs and symbols around your company tell your staff? Are you a bellwether for excellence?

What are some the ways you can take the lead in creating service professionals in your company or department?

CHAPTER 5

PERCEPTION MANAGEMENT

Discerning Customer Expectations

☐ UNDERSTOOD?
☐ ACCEPTED?
☐ PART OF DAILY PRACTICE?

The Customer's Perspective

Your service has two perspectives, based on two points of view: your customers' and your company's. From your perspective, your whole operation may be set up to provide quality product/service in a cost-effective and efficient manner. But from your customers' perspective, your service may not be efficient in the way that they need.

As a manager, understanding your service from the customers' point of view is essential. But if you are not in direct contact with customers, it is difficult to know exactly how they feel about your systems, procedures, and staff. In our seminars we use role play of specific company situations to give staff opportunities to appreciate customers' reactions.

We were working with staff of a commercial vehicle

leasing company. The situation was that of a lessee, whose truck had been involved in an accident on a major highway, and who had called the leasing company to find out what he should do. One of the vice presidents, taking the part of the lessee, had been a reluctant participant in the role play. But now he sat forward, anger in his voice.

"I really know how that customer felt," he said, and glared at his fellow players to express his frustration as the customer. "You know, I was getting damn' angry with you guys. I needed something done and you didn't understand that I had to know what I was supposed to do about my truck breaking down on the highway. And I had to know immediately. I had a real problem and you didn't seem to realize how serious it was — or want to act fast. You just kept asking me questions."

"We knew what your problem was. We were doing what we are supposed to do in those circumstances," they replied. "That's the company procedure in that situation."

"Well, if I had been that customer, I'd tell you people what I think of your so-called service," said the vice president. "I really know how that customer felt."

☆ ☆ ☆ ☆ ☆

What a profoundly significant statement! Someone on the inside of the organization, at the senior level, not usually directly concerned or in contact with customers' problems, quite suddenly realized how one of their customers might react to the company's service. He experienced his company's service from the customer's end and this changed his perceptions.

SIGNIFICANT INSIGHTS
Significant insights are lively ideas that change your way of looking at things and make you see them from a different perspective. They are usually beautifully simple, so simple that you say to yourself, "Of course! Why didn't I think of that before now?" Don't be deceived by simplicity. The most simple things can lead to elegant solutions of

enormous benefit to both you and your customers.

As a result of this role-play exercise, several significant insights surfaced in the discussion that followed:

1. The procedures and policies of a company may not be interpreted by all customers to be service. Customers' perceptions of what they need at any given time may not mesh with what the company is giving them.

2. Service is neither more nor less than what customers experience. Customers' experiences depend on the circumstances of the moment.

3. Staff may not be aware of some of their customers' service experiences and perceptions.

4. Customers' perceptions are valid. The way a company's customers perceive service is what counts.

This last may have been the most important insight of all, as well as the most difficult to accept. However, after discussion, all agreed that if customers are not satisfied with the company service or some aspect of it, they may not stay. Staff may not agree with customers' perceptions, but if customers go to a competitor, then perceptions count.

Customer Perceptions are What Count

You have probably heard someone in your company say, "That customer has it all wrong. That isn't really what happened." These are dangerous thoughts because the next logical step is to prove your customer wrong, and this creates a no-win situation. If a customer perceives something happened in a certain way, then you must accept that as a legitimate base for your problem-solving strategy.

It is the customers' perceptions that count. When you are in the business of providing quality service, you have to ensure that staff understand that the quality of your service is what customers' perceive it to be at at any given time. Then your staff will have a better understanding of the importance of every customer contact with your product and with everyone in your company. One bad experience, one unsatisfactory contact with products or employees, can change a customer's perceptions of your service from positive to negative.

Barbara Caldwell, president of CleanWear, says: "If you miss once, you may wipe out anything good you've done, no matter for how long you've done it. We are frequently judged on the time we missed, not on all the other times when we did it right. It may not be a major goof, but it's the one the customer remembers."

The critical issue here is: "What the customer remembers is what counts." The corollary is: "We must ensure that what the customer remembers is satisfaction."

Remember that service takes place between people, not between customers and companies, or shipping, or credit, or accounting. *People* move goods, *people* give or deny credit, *people* send out invoices. Not only what people do, but *how* they do it, makes customers believe they are valued and well treated. As customers, we believe we receive good service when we feel as though we count for something more than the invoice number or the check.

Any unsatisfactory contact with your company, through either your products or your people, has the potential to cause customers to re-evaluate the quality of your service or even to question your credibility. If your customers have a long-term commitment to the use of your product and/or service, they are more likely to tell you when they are dissatisfied. For instance, in our role-play situation at the beginning of this chapter, changing suppliers would entail a major upheaval for the customer, incurring disruption to business, as well as a financial penalty. But if customers can obtain similar goods or services from your competitors with little financial or physical cost, then they may become your ex-customers before you have an opportunity to talk with them.

Remember: The quality of your service is exactly what any customer, at any time, perceives it to be. That perception may be based on a one-time contact with your product or organization, or it may be the result of a number of contacts with a variety of staff. So you can see how it pays to keep in touch with your customers' perceptions.

THE INTANGIBLES OF SERVICE

A customer's perceptions are more often based on the intangibles of service than on the tangibles. The tangibles are those things that can be measured: numbers of units ordered, delivery time, defect percentage, and costs of value-added features. The intangibles are those things that are difficult to measure or quantify, such as the way company members treat their customers — the *style* of service. A customer more often reacts more to how a service is delivered than *what* is delivered. Although the perceptions built up here are the most difficult to measure and control, they are often the basis for a customer's interpretation of the way a company does business. These perceptions can have a bottom-line effect.

That is why you have to be constantly aware of the intangibles. You have to make sure the *style* of your service — *how* it is delivered by your staff — is always consistent and of top quality. This may sound as though service is a "smiles and chuckles" operation and that all you have to do is tell your employees, "Make certain customers get that smile and they will think you are terrific." But this is too simplistic an approach. Service as a fine art is more than just smiling. It is caring about the customer and the customer's perceptions.

The Fine Art of Perception Management

Successful perception management starts with identifying your customers' perceptions of your company's services and then finding out what assumptions and expectations your customer had, which were or were not met, that created these perceptions. Once you have isolated what your customers' expectations are, you can set about matching your service to your customers' needs. Then you can be assured your customers' perceptions will be positive.

The secret to perception management is to be aware that your perceptions may not always mesh with those of your customers. The manner in which people respond to each other, to circumstances, and to events is not always predictable. Two people in similar situations may have different reactions. For example, I know of one instance when a company delivered an order to a customer a day early anticipating pats on the back for promptness. In fact, the early delivery precipitated a crisis for everyone; there was no space in the warehouse so the truck could not be unloaded and the order had to be returned to its source where there were no more storage facilities. The supplier thought he was doing the customer a favor, but the customer perceived the event as an aggravation.

The moral of the story is: you can't impose your perceptions of service on your customers. As the V.P. at the beginning of the chapter discovered, you have to look at your service from your customers' business perspective.

Barbara Caldwell of CleanWear has some interesting comments.

> Service is not what you think your customers want, but what they tell you they want. It sounds simple, but of course, it isn't simple. It is actually one of the most difficult things to find out, because it can differ from customer to customer. And sometimes they don't know what they want. We spend a lot of time finding out what customers think works for them.

Successful perception management means finding out your customers' assumptions and expectations about your service.

Assumptions and Expectations

Customers' perceptions of service are based on certain expectations, which in turn are based on certain assumptions. Assumptions are statements or facts that we take for granted; they are usually unproven ideas, not necessarily based on truth, that are formed as a result of our beliefs and value systems. Expectations are the anticipation that something will occur. The assumptions we have about service lead to our expectations of the service we will receive. Whether or not our expectations of service are met will in turn influence our perceptions of a company. The following story and accompanying chart illustrate the relationship of assumptions, expectations, and perceptions.

The Case of
THE UNFULFILLED EXPECTATIONS

One Saturday, my guest and I decided to have lunch in a restaurant catering primarily to the Monday to Friday business crowd. We assumed that since the restaurant was open, they were in business as usual. We gave our order and expected that our selection would be available and appear as usual within a few minutes.

But they were not in business as usual. Our selections were not available and our final order did not appear for at least half an hour. Our basic assumption was obviously incorrect, and our expectations were unfulfilled. We did not have a happy experience, and we probably will not return to that restaurant.

If we had told the waiter that we assumed it was business as usual — or if he had told us that it wasn't business as usual — we might have restructured our expectations. The outcome would then have been satisfactory, and we would not have left with negative perceptions of the restaurant. But not many of us start out a business transaction with a discussion of our assumptions and expectations.

It's important to know your customers' assumptions, but it's not always easy to dig them out. You need to know what to ask and what to listen for.

The following illustrates the relationship between assumptions, expectations, and perceptions.

Assumptions
As a new customer, I have some broad, general, mostly unproven, ideas about your product, company, service.
Restaurant Example:
The restaurant is open — it must be business as usual.

Expectations
As a new customer, I expect some quite specific outcomes as a result of being your customer.
Restaurant Example:
I expect that I can select anything from the menu and that it will be ready shortly.

Perceptions
As a new customer I will react to your service, and form either a positive or negative perception.
Restaurant Example:
Because my selection is not available and my final order has taken far too long to prepare, I do not think much of your service and I will likely not give you my business in future.

Here is another example. A full page advertisement in a national magazine reads, "This is our 800 telephone number. Call us any time for technical support." Customers reading this ad assume that the company is open for business twenty-four hours a day. People working late on a technical problem expect that when they call that number, regardless of the time of day or night, a qualified person will be available to offer assistance. This is what the company advertises and this is what the customers expect.

If a customer calls at 2:00 A.M., and gets appropriate assistance, the outcome will be what was expected, and perceptions toward that company's service will be positive. But if the customer's call is answered by a recorded message that says, "Our hours are 8:00 A.M., to 8:00 P.M. Please leave your name and number at the sound of the tone, and we will return your call in the morning," then expectations are not met, the outcome is not satisfactory, and the customer's perceptions of service will be negative.

All customers come with a set of basic assumptions and expectations about your company, your product, the manner in which they will be treated, and the type and quality of service you will provide. They anticipate satisfactory results, or outcomes, even though they may never have truly identified or articulated their exact definition of "satisfactory" to you, or even necessarily to themselves.

Until new customers actually use your product and then contact your company, the assumptions that formed at least part of the initial purchasing decision may be unconscious. They are frequently a hidden and unspoken agenda.

As Barbara Caldwell has pointed out, "Sometimes customers don't know what they want." Customers haven't necessarily dredged their assumptions up from the unconscious. An essential element of successful perception management is designing and asking questions to bring those assumptions to the surface so that, if possible, you can meet their expectations.

As your customers receive more of your product and have more contact with various people in the company — the order desk, accounts, shipping — a business relationship develops and they experience more and more of your company's idea of service. Their perceptions of your service build. If their initial expectations are fulfilled, or even enhanced, you will have a successful partnership. But if the initial assumptions and expectations are not fulfilled and the outcomes are unsatisfactory, you will have an unhappy customer, or perhaps an ex-customer.

The case of
THE UNANSWERED TELEPHONES

Ninety percent of a certain company's business was conducted over the telephone. Since their product was quite specialized they had only one competitor.

The managers assumed that answering the telephone was not an appropriate managerial function, in spite of the fact that the company was short staffed. They not only expected others to do this job, but assumed that customers would be satisfied to wait on the line until an appropriate person picked the telephone. There was actually an unofficial betting pool among the managers based on the number of times a telephone rang before one of the support staff answered. Twenty-five times was the record win.

These managers also apparently assumed they could fulfil customers' expectations of service, and for a certain period of time they were able to do so. However, eventually customers found other sources, and business started to decrease. Customers perceived that this company apparently didn't want their business.

At this point, senior management sprang into action. All employees at all levels were told that the telephones were everyone's business. Subsequently, all staff were expected to answer by the third ring. As a result, staff assumptions and expectations of how they should behave came into line with their customers' assumptions and expectations: customers' perceptions of the company changed for the better, and business improved dramatically.

Matching Customer Expectations with Service Delivery

Customer assumptions and expectations must match the delivery of your service. You and your customers need to share and articulate assumptions so that you both have similar expectations. Unless you take the time for this sharing, there will be gaps in understanding, and negative customer perceptions may be the result. Much of perception management is making certain that both you and your customers have similar service assumptions and expectations.

To understand customers' assumptions and expectations as these relate to your service, you need to know how to ask questions and listen to responses; your ability and capacity to meet customers' service expectations, effectively and efficiently, is the key to your competitive advantage.

Barbara Caldwell explains how they help customers identify their assumptions and expectations at CleanWear.

> When we have new customers, we work with them, telling them how things work best for us and asking if this meets their needs. Can they give us two weeks lead time — or three? We want customers to understand that this really is a partnership, that we need to work together. Then they know that their expectations are also the expectations of the supplier.

If you and your customer have good communication, their assumptions and expectations about your service will match your delivery of that service. For more about communication, see chapter 6.

The twofold challenge: The first part of the challenge is to identify underlying assumptions and expectations of the service you will provide by working with your customers. Tell them what you can do. Ask them what they need. The partnership approach works best.

The second part of the challenge is to keep in touch with customers' changing assumptions and expectations. Over time there will be changes, both in their businesses and in yours. Constant communication and dialogue are the most effective methods to find out what is going on in your customers' minds. Continue to talk with your customers — your partners.

The Business Marriage: An Evolving Relationship

Business is a lot like marriage. First, there is the fun and excitement of the initial courtship of your beloved (your customer). Then, when two people have made the commitment to stay together, there is the more difficult task of making the relationship a continuing success, every day, every week, every year.

In a successful marriage, much depends on the quality of communication and understanding that exists between the two people. Relationships frequently breakdown when there is a communication gap, a mismatch of perceptions of what each needs and receives from the other. When the partners can say, "I understand how you feel when...," they have a basis for dialogue and perhaps compromise. "I can do this, but not that. What do you think?"

"Courting" and signing on new customers is certainly important and exciting, but it's only one small step in the success story. The real challenge is to keep your partner, your customer, with you, year after year, in a satisfactory, but changing, relationship. As with your marriage partner, your customer's needs will change and evolve over time. An essential part of your perception management strategy is being aware of these changing needs so you can continue to meet your customer's expectations regarding your service delivery. From time to time, you will need to reassess your customer's assumptions, expectations, and perceptions to ensure that both sides are still satisfied.

The way to maintain awareness of your customer's assumptions, expectations, and perceptions is through communication. Ask "How are we doing?" Look ahead to chapter 7 for ways to communicate with your customers. As a manager practicing perception management, you must also make certain that everyone in your department or organization understands, accepts, and uses effective communication skills. Chapter 6 outlines ways to help your staff become better communicators.

Summary

1. Your service has two perspectives: yours and your customers'. Meshing and matching these two perspectives, now and in the future, is the challenge of quality service.

2. The customers' perceptions are what count. Everyone in the company must be aware of customers' perceptions of your service. Regardless of what you think you provide as service, if the customer is dissatisfied, then you have not provided satisfactory service for that customer.

3. The intangibles, the human factors, are difficult to manage and control and are often the basis for customers' interpretations of the way you do business. Service is the art of how you do things as much as *what* you do.

4. Perception management is the art of being aware of your customers' perceptions and finding out what assumptions and expectations have led to these perceptions, in order to keep customers satisfied.

5. Customers make assumptions that lead to expectations about the way a service is delivered. Unfulfilled expec-

tations cause customers to perceive a service as unsatisfactory.

Take a Break ... Time Out

SERVICE OR INTRUSION?

Ms. Jacks arrived at the Elite Hotel to attend a two-day
conference being held in the hotel. After opening the door
of the taxi, the doorman took her luggage from the trunk,
noticing the name tags, and escorted her up the stairs. As
they entered the hotel, the doorman said, "Ms. Jacks, I will
introduce you to the bell captain, and he will have your
luggage taken up after you have registered."

Fred was assigned to take Ms. Jacks and the luggage up
to her room. After unlocking the door, turning on the
lights, and showing her where the temperature control was
located, Fred went down the hall to fill the ice bucket
although ice was not requested.

At the end of the two-day conference, Ms. Jacks left the
hotel for the first time since she had arrived.

"Good afternoon, Ms. Jacks," the doorman greeted her.
"It's very cold for walking today. Perhaps you'd like a
taxi?"

"A good example of service excellence," was Ms. Jacks'
reaction.

However, describing her experience to friends a few
days later, Ms. Jacks was surprised to hear mixed responses.

Two people felt that it was presumptuous of the doorman to address Ms. Jacks by name simply by looking at the
luggage tags. A third person agreed with Ms. Jacks that the
doorman was practicing the art of good service.

This story illustrates the dilemmas that sometimes
arise in the delivery of service. In spite of the best of
intentions, some people may not agree with your ideas of
good service.

WHO COMES FIRST?

My friend and I were customers in a very up-scale, very crowded wine store, where we had waited for thirty minutes before our turn came to be served. We were in the midst of asking the clerk's advice, and making our choices, when he was called to the telephone. Again, we waited, this time for ten minutes for him to return.

When he finally came back, we told him that we thought we had first call on his time — not someone telephoning in from outside.

"That was _____," he said naming a world-famous person, "ordering some cases of his favorite wines. You wouldn't really expect me not to take that call, would you!"

In this illustration, there is obviously a difference in the expectations for service by the customer and the delivery of service by the clerk. Was the clerk justified in putting the telephone caller first — famous or not? How would you instruct your employees to act in this kind of situation?

Take a Break ... Time Out

PERCEPTION MANAGEMENT

The first step to perception management is to step right into the customer's shoes. You can never truly understand your customers' business or their perceptions of yours until you have experienced, or at least looked at, some of their frustrations.

1. The best thing to do is to visit customers. Get a first-hand feel for the manner and style in which their business functions. Think about the impact of your product and your people on their day-to-day operations. Think about their perceptions of you. Give yourself or your staff an opportunity to gain significant insights first hand. Tell your people, when they go out

to visit, to pick up insights and not to come back without at least one.

2. If it isn't feasible for you or your staff to go out to customers, what can you do?

   a) Ask your staff questions: What did you learn about a customer this week? What questions do you think we need to ask our customers?

   b) At your next meeting, set up a role-play situation about actual incidents that have happened. Ask your staff to think of some instances where they might have handled things differently. Have one person play the part of the customer and another a staff member. At the end of the role play, ask the "customer" how she felt. Was she satisfied? What would she have changed? Write up the significant insights on a flip chart for all to see. Ask everyone what steps should be taken for a satisfactory outcome.

CHAPTER 6

COMMUNICATION

Maintaining Customer Relations

- ☐ ACCEPTED?
- ☐ UNDERSTOOD?
- ☐ PART OF DAILY PRACTICE?

Your Customer Connections: Are They in Good Condition?

Warning! Your customer connections may need a re-evaluation and an overhaul! Some of the connecting points may be ready to fall apart. When did you last have a complete check-up of your total communications system? You have regular oil changes and tire checks done on your car. Is your vital customer connection any less important?

Talk about communication systems and you'll hear all about the fantastic new technology that's been installed: computer networks that allow one computer to "talk" to other computers; electronic mail that means fewer letters to type; fax machines that give you a written reply or order on the same day; direct-in-dialing that eliminates the need for a complicated switchboard; call-forwarding that allows you to leave your desk; cellular telephones that put you in touch with anyone any time. The list is apparently endless.

But when you ask, "Did the installation of this particular technology solve all your communication problems?", feet shuffle, eyes glaze over, and someone says, "Well, there are just a few things we hadn't anticipated." When you look closely, you find the "things" are usually the people on each end of the technology. You can have all the state-of-the-art equipment in the world, but the quality of your communication still depends on people.

Technology facilitates, but it is people who activate. It is people who compose the letters and fax the messages, answer the telephones and meet with the customers. People use the devices to communicate with other people. People respond to each other across the technological links. It is the way the people in your company communicate that establishes the tone and quality of your customer connections — your customer relationships.

You hear about "communication" as though it were an abstract concept floating in the atmosphere. It is not an abstraction but a link between people — a dynamic link that is always in a state of potential change. Think of communication as the actions you and others take to ensure that your customer connections — your customer relationships — are always in excellent repair.

Communication and Social Competence

As a customer, would you stay with a company that provided poor quality service and discourteous communications? A colleague said to me the other day, "I am sick and tired of people who can't extend common courtesies to me when I get gas for my car, go to a restaurant, buy groceries, telephone for information, or attempt to do business with a company. I just don't use those places any more. Doesn't anyone know how to treat customers with a little respect?"

My colleague is not alone. If you don't like the way your supplier treats you or your people, you can look elsewhere. More and more customers choose not to remain in such situations. Competitive products and companies exist in almost every form of goods and services, so there are plenty of alternatives. You can switch suppliers of consumer goods and services relatively inexpensively.

Even in technological areas, where you may have long–term commitments with another organization, when the time comes to re-evaluate needs, you can change suppliers.

Let's look at the phrases "common courtesies" and "lack of respect" used by my colleague. Courtesy and respect are the outward evidence of some degree of social competence in a business setting. By showing courtesy and respect to one another, people demonstrate a grasp of the basic elements of social skills. They show some knowledge of appropriate behavior in personal and business situations, regardless of their private feelings. Communication skills are a large part of social skills, since communication is our main means of interacting with other people. Both are important to quality customer service.

As customers, our minimum requirement is to be treated courteously and respectfully. As business people, we should demand that the minimum requirement for any of our employees is sufficient social maturity and professionalism to handle the requirements of the job. This implies a set of standards of socially competent behavior for employees in every type of business. It also implies training where necessary to improve these skills where they are lacking. Here is a story of such training.

In the early sixties, wives were starting to attend company social functions and conferences with their husbands. Some of these functions included dancing. The president of a certain corporation realized that not all his management staff were comfortable with dancing as a social skill. So he took steps to remedy the situation.

After telling his managers that social etiquette dictated that men dance with each others wives, he brought in a dancing instructor for an hour once a week for several weeks. Instruction took place in the warehouse. As the teacher called the steps to the various dances, the managers (all men!) danced with each other and mastered the art.

Of course you smile. Styles have changed; this kind of activity no longer has the social and business significance it once had. But the lesson is the same: some people may not have the requisite social skills necessary for a particular business setting; it is the company's responsibility to ensure that they are taught.

You frequently hear customers complain that people in the front–line jobs are rude, discourteous, and simply don't care. Such people reflect the attitudes of their bosses. If the boss can't be bothered to train staff, or doesn't know how, then the fault lies there, not with the employee.

One of the gaps in our modern world seems to be a lack of knowledge, in a large segment of our population, about what constitutes etiquette and the value of courtesy. In contemporary society, many people don't have an opportunity to learn social or communication skills at home or at school. This means they have to be taught in the workplace. The teachers?—the managers. Managers must be socially competent themselves and able to teach this competence to their staff. Look at social competence as a requirement of the job.

Social competence means that you know how to handle yourself appropriately in a wide variety of situations and with people at all levels. You know how to keep your head and remain cool under the stress. When you know and use the conventions, you can get on with the real business at hand without causing a misunderstanding. Social competence is a sign of maturity and an important characteristic of a professional. All people who work in any aspect of service need to consider themselves as service professionals and conduct themselves in an appropriately professional manner. As a manager, it is your job to teach staff the rudiments of professionalism — of social competence.

Ensuring High Standards of Social Competence and Communication Skills

Staff need to know the elements of professional behavior. Below is a list of ways you can ensure your company staff are professionals with competent social and communications skills.

1. Formulate your requirements for the people you hire. What do you expect people in various jobs to be able to do? It is all too easy to assume that everyone knows what you mean. Take the time to identify and record on paper the social skills required for the job. For instance, a receptionist needs to know how to greet people in a friendly, but professional manner, both in person or over the telephone. Staff who handle complaints or irate customers must be able to work under stress and maintain the goodwill of customers.

2. Interview for the required social competence as well as for the technical skills of the job. Use open-ended questions such as: "Let's talk about the most difficult situation you have ever handled." Give them a sample situation and ask them how they would deal with it.

3. Train, train, train. Your staff needs to know and use standard etiquette appropriate to a given situation: for example, giving a salutation — "Hello, Good morning" or "Good afternoon" — rather than an abrupt, "Yes" when answering the telephone. Your staff need to understand that courtesy is professional. Role plays are an excellent method of training. A word of caution: this is not an area for amateurs. Role plays are powerful training tools but must be handled with care and sensitivity for positive results. Consider using consultants to work through the situations with you to avoid any damaging outcomes.

4. Recognize accomplishments. You can do this frequently and informally, or at set times with a formal presentation.

Requisite social skills, applicable to everyone in the organization, are based on the Golden Rule: Do unto others what you would have them do unto you. Here are a few contemporary suggestions, updated since the original formulation.

- Be respectful. Customers keep you in business.

- Be courteous, even if the world annoys you.

- Return your telephone calls.

- Let customers know if there has been a delay.

- If you don't know the answer to a question, ask someone who does, then get back to the customer as soon as you possibly can.

BENEFITS OF SOCIAL COMPETENCE

There are bottom-line benefits to training staff in the necessary social and communication skills. The lack of respect and courtesy my colleague mentioned at the beginning of the chapter has financial repercussions. A customer's feeling of "lack of respect for my business needs," can easily translate into your competitor's gain. That response can spell the end of your connection with that particular customer.

Kenneth Matheson, president of Armstrong World Industries Canada Limited, knows the need for social competence in business. One of Armstrong's corporate operating principles stresses the necessity of good taste and common courtesy in all attitudes, words, and deeds.

You may want to consider adopting a similar type of operating principle to emphasize the importance of social competence in your company's value system. Then, as with all your operating principles, make certain that all staff are familiar with the statement. As a manager, you can talk with your staff about the statement. Ask them what "good taste" and "common courtesy" mean to them in their jobs. Encourage people to think of standards that reflect taste and courtesy in everything that is done inside and outside the company. You will find that once staff begin to understand the meaning of good taste and courtesy in relation to their own jobs, they are more likely to make the necessary changes to their own conduct. (There is additional information about operating principles in chapter 9.)

The quality of your communications reflects your standards of social competence and is a critical factor in the maintenance of your competitive position. In some circumstances, discussed further on in this chapter, certain kinds of communication can give you an edge on your competition.

The Details of Communication

A friend saw the following graffiti on the subway in New York. It is not very elegant, but I think it is absolutely to the point when applied to company communications.

Don't sweat the small stuff

and underneath in large lettering:

BUT IT'S THE DETAILS THAT COUNT

Don't take chances with loose or sloppy communications. All forms of communication transmit attitudes as well as ideas and information. Your customers assess and evaluate, consciously and unconsciously, your company's attitudes and values about service and quality through the methods and details of your communications. The tenor of your communications, through writing, speaking, and behavior, conveys messages about your organization's care and concern for its customers.

Now is a good time to begin the re-evaluation of your customer connection system. It's relatively easy for technical people to assess and repair the hardware, but appraising the quality of communication requires another kind of expertise. Consider using a consultant to assist you with this critical component of quality service. Details are important.

TELEPHONE COMMUNICATION

You can't overestimate the importance of the communication that takes place over the telephone. Customers are won or lost depending on how they perceive they are treated over the telephone. Staff may not realize how important the quality of telephone communication is to the health of an organization — and to their jobs. As a manager, you may need to talk to staff about the importance of telephone skills.

Business communication over the telephone is of such importance that I have devoted all of chapter 8 to this topic.

FACE-TO-FACE COMMUNICATION

Social competence in any business setting where your people will be face-to-face with customers is absolutely necessary. Staff must know that the first priority is to make customers feel welcome and comfortable.

About sixty percent of what we "hear" when we converse face-to-face, we actually interpret through non-verbal communication such as body language. We constantly send messages to others, both verbally and non-verbally, and sometimes the non-verbal messages are not congruent with the words. An example of this is the person who says "How may I help you," as he or she continues to do another job such as writing a memo or counting cash. In cases such as these, customers will not believe that service is a priority. The message here is, "My job is more important than your business here."

Service skills in face-to-face communication must include non-verbal communication skills. Details such as how to dress, how to approach customers, when and how to make eye contact and smile are all critical to face-to-face relationships with customers. The message that goes out — verbal and non-verbal — to all customers must be: "My business is to serve you. You are my only concern at this time."

You cannot assume that people know the face-to-face communication skills. Again, this is a matter of training and of constantly reviewing expectations. Ask your staff to assist you in identifying appropriate and non-appropriate service behaviors. Involve staff in the exercise of setting standards. You may find that many people don't know the necessary social skills. They may not know how to handle difficult situations such as angry customers. People sometimes appear to be rude or discourteous simply because they do not know what to do in a particular situation.

Role playing everyday situations is an excellent way to review and teach necessary skills, both verbal and nonverbal. You can use appropriate situations for staff at a variety of levels, including management. Again a word of warning: as this type of training can raise some very sensitive issues for participants, unless you are experienced in role-playing techniques, have a consultant assist you.

WRITTEN COMMUNICATION
A critical aspect of the details of service is the quality of your written communication. Writing to customers used to be a simple matter of deciding what to say, typing the letter, signing it, and putting it in the mail. Now we have letters that go via couriers, electronic mail, and fax machines, as well as from one computer to another.

There have always been problems with letter-writing: format, spelling, typos, accuracy, poor sentence structure, unclear meaning. Although customers may receive written communications more rapidly, the quality may leave them just as, or even more, confused, annoyed, or skeptical as they were previously.

A colleague told me the other day that she has now decreased her letter writing by half since she acquired a fax machine. "A good part of the time, I now don't have to fuss with the formality of letters, or wait for my secretary to produce them. With fax, I just type in what I want to say, press the button, and off it goes. Of course, sometimes I wish I had re-read the message because I'm not sure how it will sound on the other end. But, by that time, it's gone, and there is nothing I can do about it."

With the new technology, there is even more potential for problems as you can see from the example above. You may press the button before you have thought about the receiver's reaction to your communication. There are also new kinds of errors, such as that contained in the salutation of a letter I received the other day soliciting my business.

> ANNE PETITE
> ANNE PETITE & ASSOCIATES
> 160 GUILDWOOD PARKWAY
> WEST HILL, ONTARIO
>
> DEAR SIR,

Two things annoy me about this letter: the apparent disrespect reflected in the salutation and the lack of concern for quality from a company that wants my business. At first glance, the error in the salutation seems to be just a minor glitch. This is probably a computer-generated mailing, sent out to give me important information about a product that is relevant to my work. But this example points out an important contemporary predicament. Although we can generate a greater amount of printed material more quickly than was ever possible, more time and commitment are required to ensure accuracy and quality.

I question the quality of service of this particular organization. Do they not care about the letters they send out? At what point does quality become a concern — when your order exceeds $1,000? $1,000,000? A small point perhaps, but it's these kinds of details that contribute to a customer's total perception of a company.

A minimum requirement for any company person who sends out any written communication is a dictionary and a spelling reference. Letters should be written in language appropriate to the receiver. If you are writing something for a technical person, you can use technical terms, but if the receiver is a non-technical person, avoid jargon. You never go wrong when you say what you mean in clear, simple language. Your readers, your audience, your cus-

tomers, will love you for it. Clear, simple language includes the reader immediately. Jargon is a power play that
sets up barriers to understanding.

INTERNAL COMMUNICATION

A strong organizational community that emphasizes
service as a core value needs to have excellent internal
communications. If you have ever been in the position of
trying to assist a customer with a concern, only to find that
another person in your organization has taken over the
problem but has not told you so, you will know the
frustration of poor communication. In this situation, from
your customer's point of view, the people in your company are wasting his or her valuable time.

In a large organization, it's often difficult and time
consuming to keep others informed. However, effective
communication gives you the tools to prevent misunderstanding, and to be able to anticipate and prepare.

I asked Lloyd Crawford to tell me about the kind of
internal communication that keeps United Cooperatives
of Ontario a leader in the agricultural supply business:

> Communication isn't always perfect. It
> doesn't always happen, and you have to
> really work at it. You have to keep some
> questions in your mind all the time: *Did
> I inform everyone who needs to know?
> Did I communicate all I should have
> communicated? Will I end up with a
> decision everyone can live with?*
>
> You have to think like this all the
> time so you don't miss any of the steps.
> Then you generally don't make too many
> mistakes and you don't make decisions
> in isolation.
>
> It is a lot of work, but it means that
> you don't have to go back and repeat
> and repeat.

Those are three excellent service-related questions to use daily, which apply equally to inside and outside customers. It *is* a lot of work initially, but saves time and frustration later on.

Listening

People achieve understanding through communication, but understanding does not necessarily result from communication. Even once you have paid attention to the details of written or verbal communication and can state your thoughts clearly in an organized manner, you will not have achieved mutual understanding until you have mastered the art of listening.

Service means meeting the needs of your customers, and you can only discover what these needs are by listening to what your customers have to say. Listening is the supreme act of courtesy. Listening is at least fifty percent of effective communication. But of all aspects of communicating, which includes writing, speaking, and body language, listening is probably the most underdeveloped, underused and least understood.

We all like to talk. We wait patiently for the other person to finish so we can start talking again. The thought that perhaps no one wants to listen can be devastating, but we talk anyway. Have you ever wondered how you might ensure your popularity? Stop talking. Be a good listener!

In our seminars, we frequently ask participants how many good listeners they know. Responses are always the same. Most know one or two. Two or three do not know any. Very few will say, "My boss." Almost everyone admits to needing more practice themselves.

Good listeners are obviously a rare species, and that could be a danger signal when we think about the importance of communicating with customers. Good listening skills are just as important as good writing and speaking skills when it comes to improving our customer connections.

WHAT IS LISTENING?

Listening is an action and a style of behavior. Listening is certainly much more than good hearing. One of the best listeners I know is hearing impaired. The first qualification is a sincere desire to understand what is being said to you — not just the words, but the underlying meaning. There is no greater sign of respect than taking the time to show a genuine interest in what is being said to you.

Listening is a private occupation, even when there are other people present. It takes place inside your head, and until researchers develop a means of turning mental processes into easily recognizable public images, you can keep your thoughts to yourself, and put them in any order you wish without any danger of exposure. You can listen only to the sounds, or actually hear and interpret the words and underlying meaning. You can pay attention or wander off to other vistas. Unless you have a hearing impairment, or other disability, you can choose whether to listen or not.

To be truly rewarding and effective, communicating with others is a cooperative event. But you can never be quite certain that you have the degree of cooperation you want because it's difficult to ensure that others are really listening. One of the most frustrating aspects of talking is that you don't know whether or not you are engaging the other person's full attention.

One of my school teachers used to stop in mid-sentence, look around the class room, and say to some poor soul, "Repeat my last two sentences back to me." In business, or even in most personal relationships, you can't demand that kind of instant feedback to determine the degree of listening. But you can develop some techniques for helping others to cooperate with you to be good listeners. The first and most important technique is to be an excellent listener yourself.

Listening requires preparation. You have probably had occasions when you prepared yourself to talk, but how many times have you prepared yourself to listen? When you have truly listened, you have asked questions, commented, and requested clarification until you know that you have understood the message and left no room for misunderstanding. You have taken the time to get things right the first time.

You need to clear your mind, put down what you have been doing, and open your brain to listening. That requires self-discipline. If you are by nature a multi-task person, someone who reads the mail while carrying on a telephone conversation for example, you will probably experience withdrawal symptoms as you practice attentive, focused listening. But stay with it. The results will all be positive.

Good listeners take notes. Assume that everyone has something to say that will be of interest to you: take your notebook with you everywhere and be prepared. You never know what you will hear, or who will say it.

Listening is active and involved. Concentrated listening requires high energy output. When people say they are just going to relax, sit back, and listen, you know they will not be actively listening. Service specifically requires highly active, involved listening. One of the dangers of keeping people in direct customer service jobs over a long period of time is that they have heard it all before, time after time. They tend to lose their freshness, edge, and enthusiasm to help customers through a problem.

Listening is contributory. Active, involved listening to others means responding, giving indications of interest through appropriate feedback, and clarifying until both parties have reached an understanding of the issue. Face-to-face listening means responding through body language. There is nothing more frustrating or disturbing than talking with someone who seems to be completely detached from the conversation.

Listening takes time but saves time. Think of listening as an investment of time with infinite pay-offs. Here are some immediate results of focused, attentive listening:

- Both parties understand the message. There is no ambiguity or possibility of subsequent error as a result of misunderstanding.

- People who know that you are a good listener and that

you will ask searching questions will develop the habit of clarifying their thoughts before they come to talk with you. They will come to the point quickly and will be much easier to understand. The whole process will probably be accomplished in much less time.

• Your credibility as a listener will be high, which will reflect positively on the credibility of your company and its service.

Listening Skills as Service Skills

Effective communication is a basic element of service. Since listening is at least fifty percent of effective communication, it must be perceived to be a valuable service activity by everyone in the company. You can show this both by example in your informal daily activities and by setting up planned, structured listening opportunities with staff and outside customers.

Most current books on management strategies describe the importance of listening but don't give details. Below are some tips to help you and your staff become better listeners.

STEPS TO EFFECTIVE LISTENING

1. When someone speaks to you, in person or over the telephone, put down whatever else you are doing. Focused, attentive listening is impossible when you are occupied with another task. Listening with one ear means you hear only half the message, and that may not be the critical half.

2. Make sure you are physically comfortable. Whether you are listening to others face-to-face or over the telephone, your body needs to be in a comfortable position. Have you assessed your chair and desk for comfort recently?

3. Create or choose an environment where everyone can

hear. Some locations, such as the corridor, a poorly ventilated room, or a noisy restaurant, are not conducive to comfortable listening. Comfort does not mean luxurious surroundings. But it does mean that everyone can listen without having to strain or fight distractions. Another reason to choose a comfortable listening environment is that some people have a hearing impairment they will not admit to.

4. Give yourself a break. After you have listened attentively you will feel the need to get up and stretch, because your muscles have been tensed. You have worked not only with your head, but your whole body.

5. Be aware of your biases. Biases are barriers to effective listening. Everyone has them, but few want to acknowledge them. Whether your bias is toward a person, an accent, a situation, or a customer, admit it to yourself and be aware of it. Once you've done this, you will know that every time you are in the presence of this particular circumstance, you must make an extra effort to listen attentively and objectively.

   Senior people sometimes have a bias unique to upper levels of management: that staff at the junior and clerical levels have nothing to say worth listening to. But it is these front-line people, who talk with customers and suppliers, who know where the glitches are. They know why the system isn't performing as it should. Show an interest, and you might be pleasantly surprised.

MONITORING LISTENING SKILLS

Monitor your own listening skills. How much of the time are you quiet? How much of the time are you not only quiet but attentive when others are speaking? Do you ask questions to clarify points? Do you listen to your staff? Participants in our seminars, at any level, have seldom identified a boss as a good listener, and there is a message in this perception: if you are not listening to staff, you are probably missing some valuable information. Staff are your internal customers and suppliers. They supply you with the information you need to do your job.

Listen particularly to your front-line staff. Most front-line people know how things can be improved. They can provide a wealth of ideas, many of which are not costly to implement. They are the people who have to handle customers all the time. They can tell you where the systems and the technology are at fault.

I know of several order-desk and service areas where the clerical staff are not only supposed to deal with the incoming orders and complaints, but make calls out to customers as well. Senior management insist it's essential that customers receive status reports about delays or service problems. But on every line, incoming calls are backed up, two and three at a time. There is literally not a second between completing one call and picking up the next. No system or procedure has been put in place to allow staff to take care of the listening side of the service job.

Most people in these situations are extraordinarily conscientious. They do their best, but no one at the management level takes the time to ask them how it might be done better. No wonder there is such high turnover in this type of job.

Do you listen to your outside customers? You and your customers are a partnership, and this implies a two-way dialogue. Think about listening to your next customer. What will you listen for? And what will you do with the information you accumulate?

Monitor your staff's listening skills. Do they appear to be giving the caller their full attention? Do they all listen with pen in hand, ready to write relevant information?

Are your staff under stress? Is it enough stress to be detrimental to their ability to listen? If so, what can be done about it?

At All-way Transportation, senior management are aware that their customer information operators work under considerable stress and tension for long stretches of time. To alleviate some of the strain, they decided to give their staff more frequent breaks. But staff did not like that. They found that when they spent time away from the tele-phones, they lost their edge. Staff and management dis-cussed the situation and came to the mutual conclusion that longer hours on the job each day and an additional day off would be a more constructive approach.

☆ ☆ ☆ ☆ ☆

Here is an example where the customer information operators and management talked together and came up with a mutually satisfactory agreement, a definite contrast to the frenzied order-desk situation described above.

When was the last time you asked your staff, "How can I help you to do your job better?" "What do we need to do together to give our customers better service?" and then truly listened, openly and non-defensively?

Invite your staff to talk with you as a group. If this is something new, you will find that most people will not talk freely and openly at first. You will have to build up a sense of trust within the group. They will want to be sure there will be no recriminations if they open up their hearts and minds to you and the group.

Receptive and non-defensive listening in this context isn't easy, particularly if you feel you are being criticized. Your posture, body language, and style of questioning all send signals to your staff that will either encourage or discourage their commitment to the process.

Ask your clerical staff what they hear from customers. It's amazing what people hear without realizing its impor-tance. Ask your staff what information they think would be useful for the company to know. Then involve them in the design of questions they could ask. One of the most simple, "How's business?", brings in a variety and wealth of information.

If you hear an employee complaining that something is getting in the way of doing the job well, stop, ask and *listen*. Track down the nature of the complaint and don't be satisfied with a superficial answer. There is a reason for staff complaints, and the resolution may solve a service problem. You may even catch a crisis while it is still in its infancy.

Listening means giving feedback, indicating that you've heard and appreciated what has been said. It's important for staff to see you taking action as a result of what they've said to you. Then they know that you not only listened, but listened with intent, with respect, and with purpose.

A cautionary note: when you listen, you hear a lot. A good listener knows when information should be kept confidential and makes sure that it remains so.

The more you listen attentively, the more your skills will improve. Once you understand the concept and the benefits of good listening, accept that it is a valuable service tool, and make a special effort to practice the skills every day, your relationships with both inside and outside customers will change. You will find the change a mind–opener.

Summary

1. Communication systems are only as good as the people who operate them. Communication is the link that joins you and your customers in a partnership.

2. An important aspect of customer service is treating customers with respect and courtesy. Adequate communication skills and social skills are therefore an important aspect of customer service.

3. You need to identify the appropriate social competencies your staff need for the various jobs. These should then become part of the job standards. If staff don't have these competencies and skills, you need to institute training programs.

4. Details count. All forms of communication — telephone, face-to-face, and written — need to be ap-

praised and improved to ensure good customer relations. Courteous telephone manner, appropriate body language, and careful attention to written material are all important details.

5. Listening is at least fifty percent of effective communication, which is vital for providing quality service. When you listen, make sure you give your full attention: put down whatever else you are doing, make sure that you are comfortable, and that you are in an environment where everyone can hear.

6. Listening skills are important service skills. Monitor your own listening skills and those of your staff. Set an example for your staff by practicing good listening. As your skills improve, so will your relations with your customers.

Take a Break... Time Out

MONITORING THE QUALITY OF YOUR COMMUNICATIONS

The people at Metropolitan Insurance monitor the quality of their letters to customers. President Ben Harrison explains:

> Periodically we review the information in the letters that go out to policy holders and claimants. We ask ourselves, "How would I feel if I received this letter?" It's amazing what garbage we get rid of.
>
> I'm a fanatic about accuracy. If there are any typos or transpositions, I want the letters re-done. With today's word processing, there is no excuse for those errors.
>
> It's really a simple matter. You de-

mand excellence and you will get excellence. People will rise to your expectations. There is a snowball effect. To
ignore the details is to say, "I don't care"
and then expectations will be reduced
to the lowest level of performance that
appears acceptable to senior people.

As a first step in your customer connection overhaul,
you might want to do as they do at Metropolitan Insurance.
Look closely at a random sampling of your written communications to customers, including statements, invoices,
and packing slips, as well as letters, proposals, and quotes.
Involve staff in the process and ask these questions:

- What is our standard for excellence in our written
communications?

- When customers receive this will they think of us as
excellent?

- If I were a customer receiving this communication,
how would I like it? How would I feel about it? Are the
meaning and purpose clearly stated?

- Is there any way we can improve this communication
to help our customers in their businesses?

Take a Break... Time Out

SHARPENING YOUR LISTENING SKILLS
Learning to listen takes time and practice. What do you
need to do to sharpen your skills?
Plan to listen:

- Selectively
- At specific times
- In a structured manner

- For the actual, not the expected
- Attentively, not superficially
- With curiosity and interest
- With acuity

Knowing that:

- What you hear goes through the filter of your biases. (Check out and know your biases and prejudices.)
- The world is full of amazing possibilities just waiting to be heard!

Take a Break... Time Out

PRACTICING LISTENING SKILLS

During an interview with Lloyd Crawford, regional sales manager of United Cooperatives of Ontario, I mentioned that I thought very few people know how to listen. He agreed, then went on to tell me what they did in U.C.O.

> I agree with you that listening is a hard thing to teach. Three years ago at U.C.O., we put together a service program and all staff members went through it. We started at the senior level, then filtered it down. As each level went through the program, they had to present it to the next level down.
>
> There were three different evening sessions. A large part of the program focused on the listening process. We emphasized that listening comes with practice. You keep asking yourself and your employees, "What did that customer *really* say to you?

In this company, they were not only teaching a program on service that included listening, they were practicing listening. Each level had to listen carefully in order to teach the next level.

All the management books tell you that listening is a very good thing to do, but they don't give you much practical assistance. You might consider using the material in this chapter as a resource, and asking your senior people to develop a talk from it for the next level of management. Then filter it through the company. If your company is small, you could ask one person to make a presentation to other staff.

MODERN TECHNOLOGY: IT'S ONLY AS GOOD AS THE USER

A company installed technology that linked all their sales offices across the country with Head Office. One of the reasons for doing this was to enable the regional sales managers to type their monthly reports directly into the machine. This would mean H.O. would have access to the information several days sooner than they had previously. Since this is an extremely competitive industry, time meant competitive advantage.

At first glance, this seems to be a very logical step, with cost/benefit advantage. However, there was a serious problem. None of the regional sales managers knew how to type. They not only had to compose detailed reports but cope with the key board and the various features of the machines. The quality of the sales reports was in jeopardy.

- Do your systems create or solve communication problems?

- Who does your technology serve?

- Before you install new technology, do you think about the service implications for your customers, both internal and external?

Take a Break... Time Out

AS IT HAPPENED:

We were conducting a seminar with a group of supervisors in a large multinational corporation. We were doing an exercise that centers on identifying the customer's basic needs and had reached the stage of writing responses on the flip chart for everyone to see and comment on.

The topic under discussion was respect. The group had decided that respect for all customers was a high priority attitude to develop in staff.

What were the characteristics of respect?

A list of words and phrases started to cover the page, such things as:

- keeping the customer informed

- using a partnership approach to the relationship

- remembering to use the customer's name

- calling back when you said you would

As we progressed down the page, with everyone chiming in their contributions, one of the participants spoke up.

"Look," she said, "I don't know what you people mean by respect. It sounds to me like a waste of time. When I'm a customer, I don't want respect, I want efficiency. I want to know if they've got what I want — yes or no. I want to get in and out of there fast. Never mind thinking of me as your partner, or calling me by name."

There was silence in the room.

IN YOUR COMPANY:

What would be your response if this were your employee?

If this were one of your customers talking with you, what would be your response?

CHAPTER 7

ASKING THE RIGHT QUESTIONS

- ☐ UNDERSTOOD?
- ☐ ACCEPTED?
- ☐ BASIS FOR DAILY ACTION?

> Learning how to shape the question is the *key* skill of the future. Without a question of profound significance, the answer will ring empty in your future. Shape the question before you shape the solution. If you get the question wrong, how can you get the solution right?
>
> Dr. Geraldine Kenney-Wallace
> Chairman, Science Council of Canada

The Potency of Questions

To paraphrase Dr. Kenney-Wallace's first sentence: learning how to shape questions is the key **service skill** of the future. The more finely service questions can be honed, the more clearly customers' assumptions and expecta- tions can be defined.

Questions are the greatest information retrieval system yet devised, and you can use them without any technical paraphernalia or hardware. If you ask appropriate questions and listen for the answers, the information you receive can save you immeasurable distress, trouble, and irritation. A friend of mine discovered this the hard way.

The Case of
THE FORGOTTEN QUESTION

My friend was new to politics, recently elected to a municipal office. He found that he enjoyed the political recognition. It was heady stuff to be in demand, to feel that he had attained a certain degree of status.

One of the many engagements he accepted was that of a panel member at a particular meeting with a relatively small audience. He asked a few questions about the purpose of the discussion and the nature of the audience, and was given some general information. Since he was familiar with the topic as well as the point of view, he thought no more about the meeting until the day arrived. He made some quick notes and appeared as scheduled.

As the discussion took place, the light dawned. He was there to represent the unpopular position as far as this particular group was concerned. To say the audience and the panel were hostile to his point of view and position is a gross understatement. They were there to tear him to pieces. He had not been prepared for that. He had not asked the right questions.

"Never again will I put myself in that position," he said to me after.

Two years later, he has become a seasoned politician. He's in control of his situation, he's prepared. "Now I know what questions to ask, and you can bet I ask them — always."

Many of us have been in at least one business or personal situation where, too late, we realize we should have asked more questions beforehand. When the incident is customer-related, the reputation of your company could be at stake. As this story illustrates, asking the right questions can keep you out of potential mine fields. Questions are the tools you need to retrieve the information that will put you in control.

The skill of questioning — the ability to ask the appropriate questions at the right time —is something that can, and should, be taught. Most of us learn through experience over time, but when you are in the service business, experience can be expensive.

The Power of Questions

Questions are power-pack tools. Ask the right question, and insights, significant insights, pop into your brain, dance through your thoughts, and dare you to ignore them. Significant insights are often simple; sometimes they arise with the question, sometimes from the response. Almost invariably, they lead to a change in perceptions and understanding.

The emphasis on service sometimes gives staff the impression that customers are in control, that they must always jump at customers' commands and react to customers rather than be in charge. But that's not the way Barbara Caldwell, President of CleanWear Products, sees the situation.

> "We ask our customers a lot of questions to help us — and our customers — anticipate their needs. We spend time finding out what works for them. That helps to put us in control."

The right questions at the right time can generate the

information that will put you in charge of the situation.

Questions are the hook that lures in people's ideas and creates involvement. Make a declarative statement and your audience will nod passively in agreement or disagreement. Ask a question requiring a response and you will get active participation and involvement. You may get challenges and arguments, but you will also certainly stimulate dialogue. Who devised the punctuation mark for the question? Is the hook shape symbolic?

Questions are the tools to explore and clarify customers' service assumptions and expectations. As we saw in chapter 5, assumptions and expectations are frequently in the unconscious mind, both yours and your customers'. We do not always verbalize them either to ourselves or to the other people directly involved. You want to avoid situations where a customer says to you, "But I assumed that you would..." You can do that by using judicious questions before there is an opportunity for an unpleasant incident to occur.

Questions identify possibilities for competitive advantages. You can assist customers to uncover and disclose hidden wants and needs. When needs have been identified, you can assess the cost/benefit of meshing them with the service you can provide. You could well discover the potential for a significant competitive advantage.

A good set of questions can actually become proprietary information. If your job is to solve problems for customers or clients, you learn that some questions will elicit the information that you need more effectively than others. You also learn to ask *all* the necessary questions during the first conversation.

A recent experience is a good illustration of proprietary questions. We produced a training video that showed exactly what my client's front–line staff do in their jobs, a good part of which involves both getting and giving information. In other words, the service in this function depends on asking the right questions, then acting *quickly* on the responses. Speed and accuracy are essential factors. Over a period of time, staff have developed both a set of very effective questions and an efficient manner of asking them. This gives our client a considerable competitive advantage. In this situation, the questions that staff use in their jobs are proprietary information.

The Skill of Questioning

We take the skill of questioning for granted, but a punctuation mark or a raised inflection at the end of the sentence does not guarantee the correct answer or automatic access to required information. "Quest," meaning search or exploration, forms the first part of the word "question." That is what questioning is: investigating assumptions, exploring expectations, testing perceptions, looking for new knowledge.

In fact, uncovering the answer is not nearly as difficult as composing the question. The right question can be deceptively simple but frequently requires considerable time and attention to frame and shape.

Listen to the questions skilful interviewers use. Questions are the tools of the interviewing trade. Notice how neatly those small and apparently simple questions elicit intriguing information for the audience. The term "a question of profound significance" does not mean the question is complex, difficult, or wordy. It means the question has been formulated and phrased in such a way that you elicit the kernel of information you need.

SHAPE THE QUESTION BEFORE YOU
SHAPE THE SOLUTION

Shaping questions is a rigorous process that is not nearly as much fun as working on solutions. Most of us have a general tendency to offer solutions before we've really thought about the accuracy and validity of the question. Solutions at least give a sense of action, while the exercise of developing questions often seems to be like trying to see in the dark.

In our work with clients, we find shaping questions to be one of the areas that requires much concentration of effort. Think of questions as tools to be used for specific jobs: identify what you want, then devise the questions to generate the information you need to achieve your goal.

For example, questions are useful tools to keep you on track: "What is our purpose?" "Are we achieving our goal?" When you are developing a service improvement program, use these two questions at frequent intervals to test your process and progress.

Questions can clarify thinking: "What is the requirement here?" "What is the result we need to achieve?"

Questions can identify customer needs: "What do you need from us?" "What can we provide for you?" "Is this satisfactory for both of us?"

Remember that service begins inside your company. Look at the three questions at the beginning of every chapter in this book. As these questions relate to your service policies and practices, does everyone, at all levels, in your company, division, or department answer "Yes" unequivocally to each? The answer to each is the barometer of employee commitment to service in your company.

SOME BASIC QUESTIONS

Why are we in business?

This is a question to ask frequently inside your company. Sometimes as I stand in line, waiting to give someone my money, or listen to the telephone ring ten times at the company switchboard, or try to interpret a set of instructions, I have some doubts that any of these organizations wants my business. Service, the concept of making things easy for customers, seems to be an abstraction, separated entirely from daily practice.

I have had accounts at my local bank and trust company for years. Yet whenever I see bonuses, give-aways, or added goodies advertised, they are always a reward for new customers. Long-time customers apparently don't count. Seldom do the tellers use my name, even though I am identified on the check. When you consider the cost of acquiring new accounts, giving some thought and time to established customers would seem to be worthwhile.

I have also had charge accounts with several major department stores for years. As I paid my bill the other day, I wondered to what degree these stores value their individual customer accounts: not just as an estimate of the number of dollars each customer spends per year, but as loyal customers who continue to do business with them. Large department stores face difficult times as competition from smaller, specialized retailers takes a big chunk of their market, and as Visa and Mastercard offer similar opportunities to pay over time. Yet, to my knowledge, not one of those giants has contacted long-time customers to say, "Thank you for staying with us. What can we do to make sure you continue to come back?" It makes me wonder if these companies have ever asked themselves the basic question, "Why are we in business?"

All these intangibles of service, which make customers feel of value, may be worth more to buyers than the actual dollar value of the product. Service is more than making products available to buyers and setting up some kind of system for collecting their money. It is a way of doing business in a style that meets or exceeds customers' expectations. Everyone needs to feel he or she is more than an account number.

How can I create a partnership environment so that we work together with our customers for mutual satisfaction?

This question needs to be addressed to customers. Invite your customers to communicate with you, to tell you what they think. Then be prepared to listen and respond. A letter, such as the one below, is an effective approach.

> DEAR CUSTOMER:
>
> Thank you for doing business with us. We hope that you continue to be our valued customer.

> Just to make certain that we are providing
> excellent service to our customers, we are
> reviewing our service policies. We would like
> to think that our standard of service meets or
> exceeds your expectations.
>
> We think of our customers as our partners. If
> there is anything we can improve, we want to
> hear from you. We would like to be number
> one on your list.
>
> YOURS TRULY,
>
> YOUR PARTNER, MR./MS. PRESIDENT

A letter such as this says, "You are important to us. We value your opinion. We truly want to know what you want from us."

Part of the partnership approach is identifying not only your customers' needs but also the needs of your organization so you can try to mesh them with those of your customers. Sometimes the needs of a customer may not fit with your own. In this case, you have to determine where your priorities are. Do you want to keep customers at all costs or do you want to provide a certain kind of service? Barbara Caldwell comments:

> People are demanding better service,
> but also better prices, and that's a tough
> combination to deliver because service
> costs money.
> We work very hard in this company
> on what we call "relationship selling."
> I would much rather not do business
> with people who want me to drop the
> price by a nickel. Then they go to my
> competition next time to see if he will
> drop his price by a nickel. I am much
> more interested in dealing with cus-

tomers who like our people and the way
we run our business. We think we give
them much better service in the end.
But the competition is fierce.

In the end, it comes down to a question of priorities and
also, realistically, realizing that competition is fierce.
Most goods and services are duplicated in today's market,
and this allows customers a broad choice of sources.
Buyers who are willing to do a little comparative shopping
can certainly narrow the choice down to the best price. But
when the time comes to actually make the purchase,
particularly a long-term commitment, it's the intangibles
of the partnership approach that buyers frequently perceive to be the value-added components of the product.
Price is not always the deciding factor.

What do our customers want?
If service means meeting the customers' needs and
expectations, then improving service must mean finding
out what customers need. If you go ahead with "improvements" without asking this question, you are more likely
to please yourself than to meet customer expectations.

Pitfalls
Some companies forget the partnership approach, implementing "service improvement programs" with little or no
input from the customers who will (or should) benefit.

The Case of
THE MISSING QUESTION
A national corporation decided to improve its service
image. The various departmental managers were called
together to be informed of the new company direction.
During the meeting, various senior executives talked about
the need for an improved service policy. They cited

instances where customer dissatisfaction was directly due to what the customers described as "poor service."

"This is a priority," said the vice-president of sales and marketing, and everyone nodded in agreement. "Service is our competitive edge." Again the nods of agreement. "We must have everyone thinking service improvement and we must begin now."

Immediately, the departmental managers thought about all those subordinates who needed to be improved.

"By mid-year, we want to see results," said the executive. "Go and develop a plan, and let's see some action towards improvement."

The departmental managers left the meeting and immediately took action. They knew this required staff commitment. The best tactic for commitment is involvement. The most effective way to get involvement and commitment is to call everyone together, ask them what they think, put the ideas together, and develop a course of action.

Departmental meetings were set up on a regular basis and, gradually, out of all the talk and words, some common threads of agreement emerged. Action plans developed, including an internal motivational program to make everyone aware of the new service thrust.

A committee was formed to work on the motivational program. They developed slogans, set up motivational meetings, showed films, and generally promoted service throughout the organization. Within the six-month period, a Service Improvement Program was in place and the general service attitude showed great improvement.

But within a few weeks, the corporation president received a letter from the president of one of their major accounts.

DEAR MR. SUPPLIER:

We have recently undergone a general downsizing. Since we are now operating with a reduced staff, we asked all personnel to identify and review areas that could result in cost-cutting or time-saving measures.

The results of this review show that some of your business practices result in some problems for us. As you know, our business depends on our speed and accuracy. We guarantee our customers next-day delivery. Speedy access to your service is essential for us.

But our survey shows:

1. That your switchboard puts callers on hold for up to 2 minutes — the record last week was 3 minutes — without explanation.

2. That your staff are frequently unavailable — "away from the desk" I believe is the phrase — and there seems to be no other person with the information my people require at that moment.

As we have had a satisfactory business relationship for some years, I want to give you the opportunity to correct the situation before we talk with your competition.

Yours truly,

Your friendly customer, etc.

This customer was talking about one of the intangibles of service — efficient business practice — as a condition of sale. These intangibles are very difficult to assess from inside the organization. You have to go outside — to the customers.

The new service policy, while incorporating many beneficial practices, neglected to include the most crucial method of improving customer service: asking customers what they want. Although motivational programs can improve staff awareness and performance in a general way, nothing takes the place of asking customers what they need and expect and then, from the answers you receive, designing the standards that will address their needs. As the letter indicates, there were gaps in the internal practices that were critical to customer satisfaction. If this company had asked for customers' opinions before they instituted the service program, they would not have received the letter or faced the possibility of a lost customer account.

Another pitfall is not only failing to ask what the customers' needs are, but also failing to listen or respond when these needs are brought to your attention.

The Case of
THE MISSING CHAIR

Not long ago, I took my elderly aunt shopping in a large multi-chain department store. Elderly people have special requirements: they need to sit down frequently, particularly when trying on clothes. Apparently, many department stores haven't yet grasped this fact. Finding a chair in a fitting room is often next to impossible.

A very helpful saleswoman, noticing my aunt's difficulty, searched around and finally produced a chair. It was such a considerate action, I made a point of writing down her name so I could write to the president of the chain. In the letter, I identified and congratulated the saleswoman, as well as outlining the difficulties experienced by the elderly. I suggested that since there are many older shoppers, catering to their needs would be good business — supplying a few chairs in appropriate areas would be relatively easy to do.

In his reply, the president thanked me for identifying the saleswoman, saying he would pass her name on to the right department. But there was not one word about providing amenities to the elderly — no hint that he was the least bit interested in my suggestions for improved service.

Did he hear me? Does he think all customers, including

the elderly, have value? Does he want to serve all customers, including seniors, or only those who don't cause any problems, such as needing chairs? Was he de-selecting a certain group of customers?

I've checked the store from time to time since I wrote the letter, and nothing has changed. In this case, a particular aspect of service — a chair conveniently placed — is a condition of sale. Since none is available, my aunt no longer shops there.

In these two situations, seemingly minor factors, such as people not at their desks, callers kept on hold, a missing chair, also become conditions of sale. If the companies had, in one case, *asked* their customers questions, and in the other, *listened* to the customer's suggestion, sales would not be jeopardized.

Avoid the Pitfalls: Keep Tuned to Your Customers

The best way to avoid the pitfalls illustrated in the last section is to ask your customers how your business measures up to their expectations. There are several ways to do this. Some companies use sophisticated surveys to assess their customers' satisfaction. Others write letters such as the one included in this chapter, or go out to talk with customers. As a manager, you can decide which method best suits your company: formal, informal, at frequent intervals, or yearly.

PERSON-TO-PERSON SURVEYS

Personal surveys, conducted by various staff who go out to talk with customers, are used by United Cooperatives of Ontario. Regional Sales Manager Lloyd Crawford explains:

> For the last three years, we have gone out on what we call "rural routes." We match up staff — district, head office, sales, and service — with one member of our local board of directors, and we go out for one or two days and call on farmers. We talk to them and ask them questions: What are we doing wrong? What would you like us to do differently?
>
> We get a lot of feedback and we pay attention. Most of the time it reinforces what we already knew, good and bad. But because we have taken the time to go out and ask "How are we doing?"; because we really listen to them — not just ask and close our ears — customers know we really care about them as customers.

The benefits of this kind of person-to-person survey? Head office staff find out when something is wrong with the service. They become aware of trends such as new product lines they should consider. They stay abreast of their customers' service requirements. And customers are pleased because U.C.O. people have taken time to talk with them.

YEARLY WRITTEN QUESTIONNAIRES

Some companies send all their customers a yearly formal questionnaire. Jerry Webster, Director of Systems Integration Operations, describes the type of survey used at Bull, a worldwide information systems company.

> We have been doing this survey for seven years. It covers the whole company and includes four categories: sales, hardware service, software service, and the generic overall company.

> The first three are major categories for us, and have about eleven to twelve questions each. The last generic section has three questions. Because we use this survey to give valid results for yearly comparison purposes, we cannot change a word, not even "a" to "the." Even though we know there are things we would like to improve and different questions we would like to ask, it is impossible to change the survey; if we did, the results would not be valid for comparison purposes.
>
> The results are analyzed and feedback is given to everyone concerned.

Webster explains that this survey is also an important strategic management tool.

> The results are very important at the organizational level. When I was responsible for the software service, I charted each question. And I had seven years of tracking by each question, so I could see trends. I could evaluate our progress in each area, as well as see our weak areas. I could then identify what the problems were and work to improve them.

FREQUENT WRITTEN QUESTIONNAIRES

At Metropolitan Insurance, customer satisfaction is assessed throughout the year. Periodically, they send out a survey along with a letter to policy holders, claimants, and brokers. This enables senior people to have "snapshot" pictures of the degree of customer satisfaction at intervals throughout the year.

This is not an extensive, formal customer satisfaction survey. But it is an effective means of sampling customer satisfaction in an informal manner — you can get a "feel" for the way your customers perceive your service. You can choose to do this at set intervals — for example, monthly or quarterly — with a certain category of customers or randomly with a variety of customer groups. This type of questionnaire should not be detailed — two or three questions will be sufficient — but you do need to follow a similar format each time so you will be able to monitor changing trends in the responses. You also need to plan in advance what groups will be sampled and at what intervals. Before you start this process, make certain you have a clear idea of what you need to know, what you will do with the information, and how you will respond to customers with specific complaints or suggestions.

Surveys serve multi-purpose functions. Not only do they keep the company in touch with their customers, they also show them trends and provide direction for future training needs.

Summary

1. Learning how to shape questions is the **key service skill** of the future. The more finely service questions can be honed, the more clearly customers' assumptions and expectations can be defined.

2. The right question at the right time puts you in control of the situation. Questions asked of customers can identify possibilities for competitive advantage and can be proprietary in nature.

3. Shape the question before you shape the solution. Working on the questions may not be as much fun as developing solutions, but formulating the right question is one of the most effective time savers in the long run.

4. Carefully designed surveys can provide you with crucial information about customers' needs. Customer surveys can take a variety of forms, including face-to-

face interviews and written questionnaires.

5. The results of customer satisfaction surveys can be used to identify trends as well as future staff training needs.

Take a Break... Time Out

AN INTERVIEW WITH BEN HARRISON

Here is an excerpt from an interview with Ben Harrison, President of Metropolitan Insurance.

ANNE PETITE: How do you monitor customer satisfaction?

BEN HARRISON: First, I think about my reaction as a customer. You have to start by measuring your own reactions to the environment around you. Monitor how you feel when you call an airline or other organization and the service person puts you on hold, and then keeps you on hold.

First ask yourself, "How do I feel about my experience with other companies?" Then ask, "How do we compare as a company to those other people?" And before you pat yourself on the back, do some checking. Have somebody — a friend — call in and then ask him or her, "How did you feel when you contacted my company?"

A.P.: Do you have any suggestions for other types of surveys?

B.H.: Formal customer service surveys can be pretty onerous things, so you have to be careful about that. But you can use something as informal and simple as a letter from the president, or the vice president of marketing. Include just one or two questions, for instance, "I've noticed that when I call other companies, this is the way I'm left feeling. When you call us, how do you feel?"

There are also dozens of mini-surveys that you can use. If you perceive a trend, develop a little survey that checks out that trend.

A.P.: It's interesting that you talk about "feeling." Is there ever a time when customers' feelings don't count?

B.H.: Feelings always have to be put into perspective. You can't let emotions rule your behavior. But customers always have feelings, which have to be taken into account.

- What business or organization have you been a customer of today or recently?

- How did the transaction take place: face-to-face, telephone, letter, fax?

- Did you receive good service every step of the way?

- How did you feel: neutral, valued, welcome, a nuisance?

- Have someone call into your company. Ask them how they feel about the service they received.

Take a Break... Time Out

BE A CUSTOMER:

If you were fortunate enough to receive a Dear Customer letter from:

- your bank

- your grocery store

- one of your major suppliers

what improvements in their service would you suggest?

Which of your suggestions would you make conditions of sale? A good test for finding this out is to ask yourself, "If a competitor offered one or more of my suggested improvements, would I go over to the competition?"

COMMUNICATE WITH YOUR CUSTOMER

Design a letter to send to one of your customers. What information do you need to know about your service? What questions will you ask to get the answers? Involve your staff in this exercise.

Remember: When you ask a question of your customers, be prepared to hear things you had not expected. Your customers may have a different perspective from yours. Be prepared to deal with the answers: once you have asked customers for their opinions, they expect you to respond.

CHAPTER 8

THE TELEPHONE CONNECTION

☐ UNDERSTOOD?
☐ ACCEPTED?
☐ PART OF DAILY PRACTICE?

Your Telephone Connection — a Fragile Link

Improving telephone communication is a basic step in creating a partnership approach to customer relations, regardless of what type of business or organization you are involved in. Here is a comment from Barbara Thornber, Director of Residential and Recreational Services, Y.W.C.A. of Metropolitan Toronto.

> We have a diverse mix of programs and needs: both people in difficulty who need the services of a social agency, as well as those who are looking for residential accommodations and recreational programs on a fee-for-service basis. It's very important that our people who answer the phone know how to treat everyone in a friendly and professional manner appropriate to their circumstances. Their telephone skills have to be first rate.

You and your customers or clients are in partnership; the critical link is your telephone connection. But of all the points where company practices meet individual requirements, this telephone connection is the most fragile and most vulnerable to the vagaries of human behavior.

No other device occupies such a universal and critical position in both a business and a social context. Pick up the telephone and you can start a war, give the go-ahead for a multi-million dollar merger, or chat with your neighbor. Over the telephone, you can develop a situation in which people want to continue to do business with you, or one in which they can't wait to get in touch with your competitors.

The telephone is the only piece of technology that can be used by a five year old, a head of state, or the C.E.O. of a multinational. It is certainly the only business instrument you learn to use at four or five, and continue to use without much further thought or training. In most instances, you learn the subtleties of telephone communication on the job. If you are a good learner and listener, you pick up the "right" skills and competencies, but it is probably more by luck than good management.

The telephone can be either an efficient business instrument for connecting people and ideas or a very effective device for creating distance and isolation.

Think of your reactions when you hear:

"Please hold." (In limbo forever)

"I'll transfer your call." (Bounced around a few times)

"All our lines are busy at the moment. Your call will be answered in sequence." (Far down the line)

As the caller, you have no control over the situation, other than to hang up. The voice at the other end is in charge, and you are left in isolation, waiting for someone to return and rescue you.

No other business device in common use has the potential to create environments for highly charged emotional confrontations. If you think about the implications of this for the day-to-day business telephone conversations, you realize that telephone communication skills and competencies are too important to leave to chance.

Front-line staff are the most common telephone link with the outside world. But with the advent of direct-in-dialing systems, management at any level can now take their own calls without going through a switchboard or receptionist first. The result is two categories of people who create an image of the style and practices of the organization. Two potential areas for either success or disaster.

Whoever represents your company over the telephone, at a given moment — front-line staff or management — creates the public image of your organization. Regardless of the rights or wrongs of the situation, customers' perceptions picked up during any telephone communication will affect their opinions of the quality of your service.

Your Invitation to the World

Once your company is listed in the telephone directory, you've invited the world to give you a call. Nowhere in any entry that I've seen does it say that only certain people are welcome. The listing implies that your telephones are there for any and all to call in to your company.

Unless you are in the retail, hospitality, or health-care sectors, more people are likely to come into your organization over the telephone than through the front door. The first voice a caller hears creates that caller's image of your company and its operation. The message behind the voice can say either, "You are welcome to come in. I am here to help you" or "Come in if you have to, but don't expect much to be done for you here. We are busy."

As someone calling in to an organization, you want:

- to hear clearly what is said

- to know you are at the right location

- to know you will be directed to the right person

- to be assisted by helpful, knowledgeable people

You don't want aggravations, problems, discourtesy, or time wasted. Unfortunately these are all too common.

The telephone is your front door. From the outsider's point of view, calling a business number is somewhat like walking into an unknown and unlit building. Unless someone greets and welcomes you, turns on the lights, and shows you where to go, politely, courteously and clearly, you will be lost.

Consider the following situation:

You dial the number of a company listed in the directory, and a voice at the other end mumbles something unintelligible. You inquire if this is the ABC company. The voice confirms that it is, so you ask to be put through to your destination. There is a moment of silence, then the voice comes back on:

"That line is busy. Hold, please." Immediately you are plunged into dead-air space without being given a chance to respond. You have no choice but to hold or hang up.

After another minute of silence, the voice returns and asks, "Would you like to continue holding, or call back later?"

You hold. This is your third try to contact an individual in this organization.

When your call finally goes through, another voice says, "Message center." You ask for information about the person you're trying to contact.

"This is just the message center," the voice says. "I can take your message, but I have no idea when Bob or Mary (or whoever) can call you back."

Or, your call may go through to the correct location. You ask if you are speaking with Mary, and the person taking her calls says, "She's not at her desk. Who's calling?"

Or you reach Mary's secretary, who asks, "May I tell her who is calling?"

Or you may simply be told by whoever is at the other end, "She is not in."

Does any of this sound familiar? Do you ever get fed up with the way the world seems to operate on the other end of the telephone? Do you sometimes feel as though you would like to leap over the telephone lines and tell those people how their business should be run? Does a telephone run-around ever cause you to run around to the competition?

If your answer is "Yes" to any or all of those questions, you know that the telephone is much more than a passive communication device on your desk or in your car. It's an accomplice for disaster or success.

The particular situation above would have taken place in anywhere from two to five minutes, depending on how long you've been put on hold. In that minuscule amount of time, your respect for that company is hanging in the balance. You, the caller, have had a frustrating experience, directed by unhelpful people who obviously regard calls from the outside as intrusions on their valuable time.

Let's look beyond the words and do some analysis to see what actually happened.

First: The company has been short changed. The name, the company's identification, is garbled, as though it is something to be kept hidden. As the caller, you have had your first two aggravations: you did not hear what was said, and you had to ask the identification of the company. As a result, company credibility is slightly at risk, and two people's time has been wasted.

Some time ago, we did some checking to find out how much of a receptionist's time was taken up in repeating the company name. Our receptionist friend looked after a very busy switchboard. Call followed call. Consequently, she spoke very quickly attempting to speed up the process. We asked her to keep tabs on her time for a few days. She found that every day she spent about ten minutes in total repeating the company name because callers had not heard it the first time. "What is ten minutes?" was her response.

There are roughly 255 working days in a year. If you calculate ten minutes a day per year, you have an astounding forty plus hours of wasted time. Forty hours of calls backed up unnecessarily. Forty hours of caller frustration when even one minute is too much. We showed our receptionist how clear enunciation of the company name may take a fraction more of her time, but actually saves her time over a few hours.

Second: You are given a command — "Hold, please." "Please" is tacked on, but in this case, it is not a request; you are not given the choice of whether or not you'd like to hold. A more appropriate response is to ask if you wish to be put on hold. If you don't, steps should be taken to see that your call is returned by the appropriate party.

Third: This time you are given a choice: to hold, or to take the responsibility of calling back. This is not a helpful choice, since you have already tried to make contact with this organization several times. Business etiquette dictates that it is never the caller's responsibility to call back unless that is your choice. As above, steps should be taken to have your call returned.

Fourth: You reach the Message Center, that nameless void where people send their calls when they are busy doing something else. From this blank location, a voice says, "This is *just* the message center." This is the first indication that this organization is staffed by "Justas": the people who are "Just Mary" or "Just Bob." They never have last names or take responsibility, and they give you the uneasy feeling that as "Justas" they are just passing through.

OR

Fifth: You reach the extension of the person you're trying to contact, but she's not there. The voice taking her calls asks abruptly, "Who's calling?" Not much courtesy here. You must have interrupted someone at work.

As a caller, you have two options: ask who wants to know and why, or think very quickly and come up with the magic name that you know will make the person you are looking for re-appear at her desk.

OR

Sixth: You are connected to the secretary whose business it is to screen the calls. In this case as well, you wish you had the magic name formula. Apparently only certain people are allowed into the inner sanctum. If the name is not right, you may be de-selected.

OR

Seventh: The individual you want is *not* in, and that is the final word the voice has to say to you. The implication is that Mary has much better things to do than to sit around all day waiting for your call.

You can be certain these are not fictitious or isolated incidents. Can your organization afford to take a chance that this might happen on your premises?

Customers come in over the telephone. Do they feel welcome?

Do all your people know that every telephone call is a potential customer gained, maintained, or lost? Does everyone realize that telephone calls have a direct impact on the company's finances, and on individual pay checks? Are all employees aware that every caller is to be treated with courtesy and respect?

Most of us are almost entirely dependent on telephones in our businesses, and we are also dependent on the people who take our calls or make calls on our behalf. Our dependence on the telephone is both an advantage and a hazard. The advantage is the convenience of the technology; the hazard is that people will make a mess out of the communication.

Management's problem is to minimize the hazards and to build on the advantages. There are no clear-cut differences among the various levels of staff when it comes to communicating over the telephone. There must be a common understanding and appreciation at all levels of the telephone as an instrument of business.

Contemporary business practices depend on the skilful use of the telephone. Although other sources of communication are becoming increasingly available, at present nothing equals the convenience of telephones. Systems have become more sophisticated, but the basic principles are still the same. People speak to people, people hear people. People develop perceptions and take actions as a result of what they have heard. Business gains or loses over the telephone.

Telephones: Service Danger Areas

"This telephone could be dangerous to our health" should be a company motto, installed on every telephone outlet, at every level. Each telephone represents a public contact point, and therefore a service danger area. These are the points where the people, including customers, meet your company. I use company rather than people here, because to the outside person, whoever is on your end of the line represents "the company." To a great extent, your service image as well as your product image is the result of the communication that takes place over your telephones.

If your service image is important to you and if you consider service to be one of your competitive advantages, then pay very close attention to these contact points. Designate them as "Hazardous Areas" every so often and make clear to your staff your service expectations regarding telephone etiquette. The first voice and the first few words that a caller hears set the tone for your entire operation, whether you have ten employees or two thousand.

We sometimes ask our clients what is the most time saving and, from a business point of view, most valuable technological device they have on the premises. The answers range all the way from photocopiers to fax machines, but finally settle on the computers. Telephones are taken so much for granted that people don't think of them as business instruments.

One of the most common perceptions of the telephone

is that it is an intrusion on work. How many times have you thought to yourself, or even said aloud, "If only I could get rid of that telephone, I could get some work done." When I begin to think along those lines, I remember the company that did ninety-nine percent of its business over the telephone. Telephones rang constantly on all desks from customers all over the continent. Staff used to pray for a second of peace so they could get the paperwork done. One day, a construction crew accidentally cut through some underground cables. The telephones stopped ringing. For the first hour, everyone rushed to get the paperwork caught up. For the second hour, they finished off the paperwork. For the third hour, they relaxed a little. By the time the fourth hour came around, panic had set in. Staff realized that hundreds of thousands of dollars worth of business was not coming in. The thought of pay checks becoming smaller made them realize the importance of each and every ring of the telephone.

You probably have one or two similar stories you could share with people in your organization. Stories like this can help to put ringing telephones in perspective.

Telephones are Business Instruments

A professional telephone manner and style are absolutely necessary in modern business practice. Among some senior people, there is a tendency to think that telephones are the responsibility of the lower levels and the front-line staff, and that, therefore, it isn't necessary for senior people to have anything to do with such low–level activities.

Unfortunately, this kind of thinking carries over to the other levels. When staff are aware that some senior people are less than professional on the telephone, they can see no reason for a different type of behavior for themselves. As a quick and simple example, when managers don't return calls promptly, they send a signal to staff: returning calls is not considered part of the service we offer. This frequently puts staff in very awkward situations. It is management's responsibility to set the example for staff, to introduce the standards, style and training.

We were conducting small group seminars on telephone customer service in one of our client companies. We were with the sixth group of employees from all levels, when one of the V.P.s, looking a little uncomfortable, admitted that he did not know how to use all the features on his telephone. As a matter of fact, he did not know how to use any of them.

There was silence for a few moments, then others admitted to being in a similar situation. "Where are the manuals we are supposed to have?" someone asked.

After much discussion, one manual was found in a clerk's desk drawer.

☆ ☆ ☆ ☆ ☆

The moral of the story? Those sophisticated, expensive systems are there to use to full capacity to better conduct business. It's not enough to bring in a new, sophisticated system, and assume that everyone will now use it in a new and sophisticated manner. Make certain that everyone has received proper training — even upper management.

Social Competence and Telephones

People who answer business telephones, or who meet the public face-to-face, require a high degree of social competence and knowledge of standard business etiquette. Since it is usually front-line staff who are in this position, all front-line staff need well-defined social competence skills. This should be one of the job requirements. Staff who do the hiring need to know how to interview for social competence as one of the necessary job-related skills.

The knowledge and use of standard etiquette enables you to gain a positive response from the other person, which gives you professional control of a situation. This is certainly true in telephone communication, particularly when you are dealing with an irate caller.

Employees are not interested in changing their manner or style unless they see reason and benefit for doing so. Management's function is to show them the reasons, then teach them what to do. Telephone social competence is a business skill essential to modern times.

Here are some points of standard telephone etiquette for a professional image. These points apply to everyone in the organization. Use this approach for all calls unless you know it is from someone in the next office.

- Speak clearly. Use a salutation such as Good Morning or Good Afternoon. No two voices are the same. Using a salutation enables callers to tune into your voice so they can hear the important things that follow.

- Identify your department or company. Callers want to know they are in the right location, and you don't know how many times this caller may have been transferred before you picked up your telephone.

- Identify yourself, using your full name. This gives you position, credibility, authority. It sets the tone for a professional approach to whatever comes next. Callers know they are not addressing a Justa.

This is what you say when you take an incoming call: "Good morning. Accounting. Mary Jones." "Good afternoon. Credit department. Bob Smith."

If you aren't used to this, you'll probably think this is too much to say. Don't think of yourself, think of your customers. Most people will appreciate this correct information. We have had hundreds of clients, at all levels, tell us this system really works. Many people call us back to tell us they can't believe how this has improved customers' attitudes towards them. It is truly the professional approach.

TIPS ON TELEPHONE ETIQUETTE TO PASS ON TO
YOUR EMPLOYEES:

The tips below about general telephone etiquette and
handling complaints are quite straightforward. You can
say to staff, "These are the standards; this is the professional approach to telephone communication. People who
behave in this manner give the message that we operate as
professionals in this company. They give us an edge."

General Tips

*   Always listen with a pencil in hand. Take notes as you
    listen. If you don't need the information, discard it at
    the end of the conversation. Taking notes helps you to
    focus on what the caller is saying — it's a good listening
    technique.

*   When you transfer a call, always give the caller the
    name of the department, as well as the person's name,
    if you know it. There are two reasons for this:

    1) If the caller is cut off, she knows who or what to ask
        for when she calls back.

    2) The caller will know he has arrived at the correct
        department when he hears the person's name.

        Say to the caller: "I will transfer your call to the
        XYZ department." Speak distinctly so the caller
        hears the complete sentence.

        If the caller is irate or complaining about some-
        thing, it's a good idea to give that information to the
        person taking the call — pleasantly and discreetly
        — before you transfer the call.

*   When the caller requests information, listen carefully
    to the request. If it is necessary to transfer the call, you
    want to be certain it goes to the right place. It's frustrat-
    ing to the caller to be bounced from department to
    department — this promotes an antagonistic relation-
    ship.

If you must search for information, tell the caller how long it will take you to find it. Give the caller a choice: to hold — or to be called back. It is never the caller's responsibility to call back, but if she chooses to call back, tell her when the best time would be for her to get that information.

- To the caller, thirty seconds on hold seems like an eternity. If you must put someone on hold, tell him how long you expect the wait to be or get back to him every thirty seconds and ask if he wishes to continue holding. This will reassure the caller that he hasn't been forgotten.

- When you take messages for others, remember to get all the essential information:

  1) **Name** — check the correct spelling with the caller

  2) **Telephone number** — read back to caller to check for accuracy

  3) **Address if appropriate** — read back to check accuracy

  4) **Message** — read back to check accuracy

  5) **Date and time of call**

  Messages are critical. Details count. Careers rise — or fall — on the accuracy of a single message. The Golden Rule applies here: take the message in the way you would like one taken for you, with all the information present and accurate. There is nothing more frustrating than an illegible or inaccurate message. **Use readable handwriting** — *please!* Don't let people get away without giving you a telephone number. Don't accept, "He knows my number" or "She knows who Jo is." Tell the caller: "She may be out of the office when she calls for messages and won't have your number with her" or "He insists that I always get a last name."

  I remember receiving a message for me to telephone Debbie. When I returned the call, I was told there were three Debbies in the company — which did I want?

- Use the caller's name once or twice in the conversation. This is a pleasant personal touch and lets the caller know she is more than just a number or voice over the telephone.

- When you end the conversation say: "Thank you for calling us, _____ (caller's name). Goodbye."

    Saying "goodbye" gives a feeling of closure and both sides know that the call is completed. A telephone call without a goodbye is like a sentence without a period.

    Saying "thank you" tells the caller you value him and appreciate his call.

Tips for Handling Complaints

- Saying "thank you" is particularly important when the call has been a complaint. You can say something like this: "Thank you for bringing this to our attention, _____ (Use the caller's name here). We appreciate the opportunity to correct the situation."

- Do not give out more information than is necessary. Callers want to know *only* when they will receive the product or the information, and the cost. Information that is not relevant to the customer's situation includes:

    1) Who was responsible for the error. (This includes your problems with your supplier as well as with people in your own company.)

    2) The number of complaints you have had about a product or service.

    3) The number of similar or other breakdowns or defects of the product.

    4) The number of employees who are on holiday or who have had flu and caused slow downs.

    5) Who has left the office early, or has not yet returned from lunch, or has not come in yet this morning.

    There is more information on handling complaints at the end of this chapter.

THE GREY AREA OF TELEPHONE ETIQUETTE

There are many aspects that are not as clear-cut as the tips listed above. The manner in which these situations are handled depends on your organization's basic value system and operating philosophy.

Call Screening

The key question is: to screen or not to screen? Do you believe that everyone in your organization should be available to all the public or only to your customers? This is indeed an area of considerable controversy. Your answer will come from your operating philosophy and will identify the manner in which you want your telephones answered. It will also determine how staff at all levels treat people over the telephone. It will be the image you present to the outside world. There are hazards to both approaches.

Here are the comments of people who believe in call screening.

- "My secretary takes the name and telephone number of callers when I'm too busy to answer. When I return the call, I can then give that person my full attention."

- "My work is to solve our customers' problems. If I answered each call as it came in, then I would never be able to complete the job I'm working on. That would really infuriate our customers."

- "Many of the people who call me are just going to get "No" for an answer. My secretary can tell them very courteously that they should not waste their time trying to get me."

- "That's what secretaries do for you. Find out who is calling and keep out people who have no business with you, so you can get your work done."

- "I just tell the secretary to take a message, and I'll return the call as soon as I have time."

Mr J.R. Grand, President of Grand and Toy, a very successful office supply company with outlets across the country, presents the opposite point of view.

> I take my own phone calls. When people call me, they want to talk with me, not an intermediary. When I telephone someone, I find it annoying to be asked, "Who is calling?"
>
> We have been in the service business since our original store was started by my great grandfather in 1882. I believe that too many people become full of their own importance. They forget why they are there. Your customer is your boss, and don't forget that.

What is your response to those comments?

If you believe that you must have the caller identified, please do it in such a way that the caller does not feel screened. You know your own business and situations best, so work with your group of people to test out various responses. Try some role play and take the callers' perceptions into account. They are the final judges of the value of your responses.

I know of one financial institution that has recently lost a customer. Every time the customer telephoned this company he was asked, "Who is calling, please?" His final response was, "It doesn't matter who is calling. I want to speak with so-and-so who happens to have my account at this time." Where do customers fit in this business scheme?

Telephone Manner and Style

This is another "grey" area, difficult to quantify. This is where social competency skills come into focus. You are not only dealing with the rules of social behavior, but social sensitivity.

Each of us develops a style of communicating. Skilful business communicators know that the manner in which they communicate is as important as what they say. If you think this is an overstatement, try this. Smile broadly, look happy, and say to someone in a very enthusiastic and cheerful tone of voice, "I've just lost my best key account. I think I might be fired!" Do you think you will be taken seriously? Your manner of presentation speaks louder than your words.

Over the telephone, about sixty percent of the message you hear is through the tone, pitch, and pace of the other person's voice. You hear as much through style and manner as you hear through the actual words.

Remember: A professional style and manner includes knowing how to use the tone, pitch, and pace of your voice to achieve a result. You know customers' perceptions of your service over the telephone depend on how you say things as much as on what you say.

Telephone Complaints

An extremely important and sensitive aspect of service is customer complaints. Excellent telephone systems mean that you can hear from unhappy customers from anywhere in the world as soon as they detect a problem. Some customers do write letters, but you will hear from the vast majority over the telephone. That is, if you hear from them at all. Most dissatisfied customers go off to another supplier.

Some companies have institutionalized complaints by routing that sort of communication through special departments, such as Customer Service or Public Relations. Staff there are specially trained to find solutions. They will take your problem through the proper channels, then come back to you with the answers. This certainly saves other people much time and many difficult conversations with irate people. The drawback to this approach is that the people who are most closely concerned with the problem in the first place never have contact with the customer who was directly affected.

COMPLAINT MANAGEMENT — A CRITICAL FACTOR

Although it cannot be covered in any depth in this book, complaint management is an essential component of a service improvement program; one of the goals of such a program should be to examine the whole complaint process to find out how customers can be better served. The first objective should be that customers have less to complain about. Another, more short-term objective, could be to decrease the number of complaints that escalate to the executive level. This latter objective was actually met in a large manufacturing company as a result of a telephone service training program for customer service staff. After a training seminar, the number of letters to the president decreased from several a month to zero.

When people take the time to complain, breathe a sigh of relief, and say thank you for calling. If they didn't complain, you would never know that something was wrong. When customers do complain, it is probably because they would rather stay with you than change to a competitor. They are giving you the opportunity to set things right.

When customers complain, listen with your head and your heart, together, simultaneously, at the same time! You listen with your head to get to the root of the problem. You ask the right questions, you record the information. You get back to them immediately if a follow-up is needed. You tell them what you are going to do, and when. You tell them what they can expect and when. Then you follow through.

At the same time, you listen with your heart because you know that frustration is an emotional response. The more frustration, the more emotional your customer will be. Something is wrong and you are being asked to fix it. Your style, your manner, and your voice tell customers that you empathize, that you understand the inconvenience. You appreciate their circumstances. Handling complaints with both your head and your heart ensures that the problem is dealt with efficiently and that the customer knows you care.

"If Alexander Graham Bell had to handle complaints, he would never have invented the telephone!" These were Ruth Haehnel's thoughts as she fielded calls from angry parents during an elementary teachers' strike. At the time, Ruth was a school trustee, an elected official with a local Board of Education.

Ruth and I have been running seminars on handling complaints and difficult people for some time, so Ruth was certainly familiar with the principles. But it wasn't until she had to deal with angry parents that she had an opportunity to test them out in such emotional circumstances. As a result of over one hundred very angry, emotionally charged calls, Ruth was able to say, "Everything we've taught really works, even under these circumstances.

"The strike was a very stressful time for everyone concerned: school board officials, trustees, teachers, parents, and children. Emotions were running very high on all sides. It was a super-charged environment with the potential for disastrous results.

"As I talked with parents, I found two things were key. The first was listening. People felt frustrated and they wanted to know they had been heard. A lot of people started off with, 'Of course, you've heard all this before, and you don't want to hear it again.' And I said, 'But I haven't heard it from you and if it is important enough for you to phone me, I have as much time as you need.' I kept my voice and tone calm and empathetic. I always smiled when I said it. Instantly you could sense a change in people. The tenor of their voices changed. They believed instantly that I was going to listen to them.

"I said to them, 'I hope that you don't mind that I'm taking notes because I want to be sure to get all the points down on paper.'

"This had the effect of calming them down, and it kept me focused and interested in the conversation, because the reality is that you *have* heard it twenty-five times before.

"The other thing that was absolutely key was tone of voice — sounding receptive, open, interested, and friendly. I believe that people knew that I really did care about their feelings. I was not giving them the brush off. It was not a parent talking to a trustee, but a person talking to a person.

"Then when we actually started to talk about issues, there was a common ground of understanding on which we could meet. They would then listen to me. The time I spent listening was an investment, because we were able to settle things in the first call, without escalating the issues. This happened because I took the time to establish a good relationship. I was able to establish a bank of trust. This was also good for the School Board. That feeling of trust carried over to their relationship with the Board."

Exactly the same techniques and principles apply when you are dealing with angry customers. You listen. You let the person know you are listening. You establish a rapport of mutual trust. You recognize and appreciate your customer's frustration. You deal with the issues from the customer's point of view. You establish a bank of goodwill and trust for the future.

As Ruth said, her experience showed these techniques work. The result is a partnership that gives you a common ground from which to tackle the issues.

Summary

1. Your company telephones are your link with customers. The people who take calls, at any level, depict the company's image to the outside world. This fragile link

is frequently in danger of damaging your service image.

2. The company number listed in the telephone directory is an invitation to anyone and everyone to call. Every conversation, regardless of its length, is a potential customer gained, maintained, or lost. Customers need to feel welcome when they telephone your organization.

3. Everyone in your company needs to know and use appropriate telephone skills and etiquette. Where these skills are lacking, management needs to implement training programs.

4. A professional style and manner of speaking on the telephone includes knowing how to use the tone, pitch, and pace of your voice to achieve results. Your customers' perceptions of your service over the telephone depend on how you say things as well as what you say.

5. Complaints are a valuable opportunity to listen to customers. Listen with both your head and your heart to ensure that the problem is dealt with efficiently and the customer knows that you care.

Take a Break... Time Out

AS IT HAPPENED:

I telephoned the office of one of the senior managers of a large financial corporation not long ago. The telephone rang and rang — I counted twenty rings — before anyone answered. When I finally reached someone, I was told the vice-president was out, and his secretary was probably out doing something with him!

Would you give that company your money to manage?

Who is responsible for the message that goes out to the public?

IN YOUR COMPANY:

What messages are your customers receiving when they call in to your company or department?

TESTING YOUR COMPANY'S RECEPTION

It may sound strange, but have you ever thought of disguising yourself as a customer to test the reception you would get in your company:

- If you had a speech impediment?
- If you had a heavy accent?
- If you sounded angry?
- If you were a small account?

If you were a potential customer in any of these cases, would you give your company your business?

CHAPTER 9

IMPLEMENTING A SERVICE IMPROVEMENT PROGRAM

☐ UNDERSTOOD?
☐ ACCEPTED?
☐ PART OF DAILY PRACTICE?

> The first thing that every business has to do right the first time, every time, is to satisfy customers.
>
> KENNETH MATHESON, PRESIDENT
> ARMSTRONG WORLD INDUSTRIES
> CANADA LIMITED

Quality and Excellence

When service improvement programs appear on the agenda, quality and excellence are frequently set out as the ultimate goals. These words have a stirring sound, the sort of bells and whistles language you use to generate enthusiasm among the troops. The hazard here is that everyone will nod in agreement as you talk, then go back to the same old routines as your inspiring discourse fades from memory.

I used the term "hazard" deliberately. The terms "quality service" and "achieving excellence" are dangerous if you use them indiscriminately. They look nice on a poster, but used without an understanding of their application to day-to-day job functions, they soon lose their punch.

Both quality and excellence are quantifiable. Each term can be identified and measured using standards set out for your product, staff, department, and company. You then assess quality and excellence in terms of those standards.

Quality service is not synonymous with luxury, nor is it descriptive or anecdotal. Rather it is prescriptive; that is, it identifies how closely you meet your service standards as well as your customers' service requirements. If your customers are those who want luxury quality, then that is what your service standards should reflect. If you are catering to the stripped-down, no-added features customer group, then you develop service standards to meet those requirements. In both cases, if you meet your standards, you are delivering quality service because you are giving customers what they require — and what they are willing to pay for. Excellence means that the standards are met or exceeded consistently.

Once you have defined and described the requirements of your service — luxury, utility or something in between — you can set standards for your company. Then you will have to consider each department separately and as part of the whole.

Any service improvement program will be successful only if it is built on standards reflecting a company philosophy that emphasizes the importance of customer satisfaction. Service must be "lived" throughout the organization as an essential component of the company culture, and not just be a topic of conversation.

SERVICE IS NOW AND FOR THE FUTURE

In the increasingly competitive and service-oriented future, there is no room for companies who give less rather than more. I would like to think that the vice president who told me, "We have looked at the quality of service we will offer — adequate, good and excellent — and we have decided to strive for adequate," represents a very small and shrinking minority.

Ben Harrison, of Metropolitan Insurance, has some very firm opinions about the impact of today's commitment on future outcomes.

> We must be seriously concerned about not just taking care of today's service problems, but anticipating those of the future. If you have a future, you had better be committed to paving the way to that future.

Competitive companies know that the quality of service today is critical to success tomorrow.

As a customer, you have certain essential service requirements for the present and for the long term. Whether you are buying a toaster or an office automation system, you need to be assured of the following:

- **Predictability and consistency:** systems, policies, and procedures are firmly in place to assure that the standards of operation and quality of product will be maintained.

- **Reliability:** the organization and the product are trustworthy.

- **Fairness:** the arrangement is equitable for both buyer and supplier.

- **Continuity:** policies, systems, and personnel are part of an overall and recognizable long-term plan.

- **Stability:** management is sound.

A successful service improvement program will be built on these requirements. The implementation of such a program requires dedication, commitment, and a high level of energy from everyone.

Developing a Fundamental Operating Principle and Policies

A successful service improvement program starts with a fundamental operating principle, which then provides guidance for the development of your operating and service policies. A principle is a general truth or law. A policy is a specific course of action developed from the principle.

As you develop policies and procedures, you look at them in relation to your operating principle. If they are not a good fit, you discard them, because effective policies must be congruent with principles. In other words, once you have a principle as the benchmark, or point of reference, you can say of your policies, "This is right," or "This is wrong."

The first task to introducing a service improvement program, then, is to write an operating principle that relates to service and to develop policies from this principle that will provide the basis for a quality service improvement program.

Outlining an entire program would require considerably more space than is available in this book. However, through the experiences of two companies, I will highlight the topics covered in the preceding chapters. The first experience illustrates how one company began the process of developing a service improvement program, including the creation of a "service-related" operating principle. The second experience outlines, through the comments of the president, how a company, now in its program's fifth year, employs strategies for maintaining such a program.

Experience Number One: Getting Started

One of our clients is a well established, small company that imports and re-packages highly technical goods. Their success has been due not only to the quality of their goods and their technical expertise, but to the excellence of service they have provided to their customers across the country.

Demands for their products have escalated in the last two years, and the number of employees has doubled to forty. Suddenly, they were confronted with the problems of success: new staff did not seem to have the same understanding of the service customers had become accustomed to; senior people felt removed from day-to-day operations and didn't know staff as well as they did previously. Service seemed to be slipping.

Up to the present, the company has operated in an informal manner without written principles, policies, or procedures. It was assumed that all employees knew the company's style of operation and expectations of them. Now, that assumption is no longer valid. The president and three senior people decided the time had come to take action. They knew that they needed some formal statements or principles that all employees could understand and accept.

This is how we suggested they proceed. We asked them to start with the quiz which you will find at the end of the chapter. This helped them to clarify some of their ideas about service and expectations of what a service improvement program might entail in their company.

John, the president, Maxine, the financial person, Susan in charge of marketing and sales, and Howard, who looks after operations, met with us for a preliminary discussion. The following scenario is a very condensed version of some of the meetings.

Although all knew that service improvement was critical, their perceptions of the actual program and the process of implementation were certainly not the same.

"I know that service improvement is not something you can accomplish overnight," John led off, "but after I finished the quiz, I began to wonder how long it will take us to to reach our goal."

"We have had an excellent reputation for service and

we still have some of the old-timers with us, so I don't see why we have to have some long, drawn-out program inflicted on us," complained Maxine.

Susan leaned forward to make her point. She obviously felt strongly. "Look at question number five — service improvement is a long-range, attitude-changing program. I really believe that's true — both that it is long range and that it means changing attitudes. We certainly need some attitude changing around here. I'm beginning to think that some of our new employees think that service is a dirty word. I don't think we can change things overnight."

"I think I agree with you, Susan," said Howard. "If we could get people to see that what they do has a direct affect on customer satisfaction, and therefore on job security and company profits, then they might start taking a more positive attitude towards service and customer satisfaction."

"That's beginning to sound like profit-sharing and bonuses," warned Maxine. "We had better think carefully about that."

Howard replied, "Question eight raises some interesting points about finances, Maxine. For example, if everyone in packaging understood and accepted that customer satisfaction depends on doing everything right the first time, can you imagine what our savings might be? We could afford some bonuses."

"I think a discussion of profit-sharing and bonuses is premature at this point," said John. "What I am beginning to see is that service improvement might not only help us to maintain our present position, but perhaps decrease costs."

More discussion took place and gradually they decided to accept the fact that service improvement was a long-term program, and that they were willing to commit themselves to the process.

"We need something to start from — a reference point," said Susan.

We explained that operating principles would provide

a reference point and act as a set of guidelines for company policies. The truly effective operating principle is vision-ary — it tells everyone what your aspirations are. In your company, you will want to have several, but in this situation, we suggested they concentrate on one that would state their vision and aspirations.

We covered several flip-chart pages with suggestions and ideas. The group agreed on some things and actively disagreed on others. But finally, this statement emerged as a viable operating principle: *To serve all our customers in an ethical, fair, and courteous manner to ensure customer satisfaction with all aspects of our company at all times.*

"Where should we go from here?" Susan asked. " I can think of several questions we need to ask ourselves."

John stood up, and taking a new sheet of flip chart paper, wrote at the top, "Policies." "That's where we are now. We have to identify some policies that will assist us to make certain that service and customer satisfaction are number one goals in this company."

Then he wrote: What must our policy be to ensure the principle of customer satisfaction with our company at all times?

Howard suggested the policy of doing things right the first time. We could see some apprehension about the implications of this idea, but also some acceptance that this might be a viable policy. Finally, the group decided that this is what should be recorded on the flip chart: Policy #1 — *right the first time, every time.*

Susan asked, "Who in the company does this policy apply to?"

"Everyone in the company." John said. "And that applies to all of us. The staff have to see that we are committed to this as well. We can't say one thing, then do another."

There were a few moments of silence while the group absorbed the implications of John's statement. Again, we were aware of some apprehensions.

Then Susan asked, "What if, despite all our efforts to do it right the first time, something happens that results in customer dissatisfaction? Always doing things right the first time may be a little heavy for some people!"

As the group considered this question, John referred back to the operating principle. He pointed out that by accepting that statement, they were then obligated to make certain that everything in their power was done to satisfy the customer. Policy #2 became *customer satisfaction.*

By the end of the meeting, they had identified two more policies and the page of the flip chart looked like this:

Operating Principle: *To serve all our customers in an ethical, fair, and courteous manner to ensure customer satisfaction with all aspects of our company at all times.*

Policies:

1. Do things right the first time, every time.
2. Do everything we possibly can to satisfy customers (within the limits of the principle).
3. Identify sources of customer dissatisfaction in order to take corrective action.
4. Involve staff in any problem solving.

All agreed that the policies were supported by the principle and that their implementation would contribute to service improvement.

We suggested that before they met again, they needed to think about the following four questions:

1. Who are our "Customers?"
2. How do we monitor customer satisfaction?
3. What specifically do we have to do right the first time to produce customer satisfaction?
4. Who is responsible for doing things right the first time?

The meeting then came to an end for the day with the understanding that they would get together the following day to address those four questions.

As you can see, this is not a quick, succinct process. Even though you may be tempted to cut short this part of the exercise, don't do so. It is crucial to make certain that everyone starts with similar interpretations of the issues. For example: Does everyone agree that service improvement is a long-term program? Does everyone agree that service improvement is a senior management intiative?

1. *Who are our customers?*

The next day they discussed the first question and, at our suggestion, decided to consider customers from the broad perspective of anyone having any contact with their product or company. This included not only the people who buy their product, but also staff, suppliers, distributors, trades people, lawyers, accountants and other outside professionals, and people seeking employment.

As we recorded the customer groupings on the flip chart, Howard leaned forward and said, "You know, I just remembered something I heard at the order desk yesterday. One of the people said, 'Oh, that's not a customer phoning. That's just one of the people in packaging. He can wait.' At the time, I didn't think that was a very bright comment, but I didn't realize what the implications for service are if staff — or any of us — think that way."

"I guess we will have to really educate ourselves and staff to think of customers as people other than those who actually use our products," remarked Maxine.

"When I look back at our operating principle and notice the "courtesy" part, I realize that perhaps some staff are not as professional as they ought to be," said Susan.

"That probably means some staff training," said Maxine.

At this point, we suggested that staff training was somewhat premature. Staff really needed to understand the concept of internal customer relationships — staff as customers of each other. When people understand that everyone in a company is both supplier and customer of other employees — using and generating information — then they begin to show a more professional and service-oriented manner towards the needs of others. Before going on to answer the next three questions the group felt it was time to present the service improvement program to junior and clerical staff.

INTRODUCING THE SERVICE IMPROVEMENT PROGRAM TO STAFF

In introducing the program to staff, the group decided to focus on two important concepts: 1)everyone in the company is a customer of someone else and 2)do things right the first time. John would introduce the new program at a meeting within the next few days. This would be followed by department meetings, as well as a session conducted by Ruth, my associate. Below is an outline of the session, covering the two concepts listed above.

Staff Session

Ruth started out by saying, "Your president has already explained the need for top quality service to remain competitive in the market. That is the reason for introducing a service improvement program — to look at all areas in the company to see how things could be done better. Everyone in the company will be taking part. As a matter of fact, all the senior people have already started working on some aspects of the program, which you will be hearing about later."

At this point, she knew that some people would be sighing and thinking to themselves: "Here we go again. Something more they've decided we should do."

She continued, knowing what the unspoken thoughts were. "Everyone will be doing something very simple in this program. It is this — everyone is going to *do things right the first time.* That applies to everyone in the company, at every level."

"Of course," some people said. "That makes sense. That's exactly what we try to do."

The critical word here is "**try.**"

"What do you mean, try?" Ruth asked.

Explanations varied.

"Well, there is always something that happens. Things get in the way."

"I never get the slips from the order department on time."

"Someone makes a mistake on the invoice form and you have to send it back."

Ruth wrote the statements on the flip-chart. "Let's look at these things that happen — the things that stop you from doing things right the first time. All these comments seem to have something in common. Any ideas?"

There were suggestions such as, "They're all communication problems" or "If only they would do this, then I could do that," but quite quickly, most people realized that the common link is that each problem seems to be caused by someone else.

Ruth pointed out that apparently no one has any control at all over his or her own destiny or job in the company. "If only the next person could be perfect, that would be the end of every problem!"

At this point, people started thinking of ways out of the situation. They began to recognize that what was perceived as a "communication problem" is really a symptom of a more basic problem — a lack of understanding of what each person needs from others and why.

In your own company or department, this is the time to introduce the idea that each person in the company is a customer of at least one other individual. Each person generates and uses information and resources critical to the efficient performance of another person. Everyone is part of the business community, working together to make quality service a reality.

As a manager, you can make certain that everyone knows who his or her internal customers or suppliers are, as well as where they fit in the information flow. Set up opportunities for staff to become familiar with the requirements of each other's jobs, so everyone knows why those papers are needed by 9:05 every morning — and not 10:00.

At the end of a session with staff, such as the one described above, your people will go away to think about the questions raised. The answers will start coming: they know what needs to be done because they are the people who are on the front line. As part of the plan, arrange opportunities to hear the answers, to help people implement the solutions. Plan also to recognize contributions. Everyone needs to have a sense of worth, an awareness that contributions have some significance. If staff are expected to behave in a professional manner, then they must be recognized in a professional style. In addition, everyone has to feel as though he or she has an active part in the process for the program to be successful. See chapter 3 for ideas about creating a sense of involvement for staff.

In summary, to make the above exercise with staff an unqualified success:

- It must be part of your comprehensive and long term plan (on paper).

- Your people must know that you are prepared to listen to them with respect, not just now, but on into the future.

- All ideas must be acknowledged and action seen to take place as a result of this staff involvement.

- An on-going recognition plan must be in place.

2. *How Do We Monitor Customer Satisfaction?*
Two weeks later, the senior management group met to discuss the issue of monitoring customer satisfaction. They determined to concentrate on the two primary categories of customers: staff members and the people who buy the company's products.

To assess internal customer satisfaction, they planned to ask staff three questions: "What do you like best about working here? What do you like least? What could be improved? All the responses were to be directed to John, who would set up a system to ensure confidentiality. Later he would report the results back to staff without identifying sources.

"This was done in another company I know of," said John. "There was a tremendous response and they were able to make positive changes, most of which were quite inexpensive to implement.

"We will have to acknowledge all the suggestions," he

explained further, "even though we may not be able to implement everything. Otherwise we will lose credibility with staff."

John had made an excellent point. Staff need to perceive that senior management is completely credible — that they follow their own example.

Later, we made some suggestions about monitoring the satisfaction of external customers. You will find information on this topic in chapter 7.

3. What is it That We Have to do Right?

An improvement program implies standards. Improvement must be quantifiable, not a fuzzy expression of ultimate hope. The requirements for specific functions must be identified in order to set standards of performance. If people are to do everything right every time, requirements must be identified in measurable terms.

"Our next task is to decide what standards we will use and how we will identify them. That will be the topic of our next meeting," said John. "That is where we can involve staff directly in the program. Their input will be essential to the process. That is our Policy #4 in action — involving staff in the problem solving process."

John and Maxine volunteered to develop a plan for staff involvement. The goal of this part of the program would be to involve staff in identifying the individual requirements of doing things right the first time.

4. Who Has to do the Right Things Right the First Time?

"We, the senior people in this organization, must lead the way," John said. "Staff have to see that we take this whole process seriously for ourselves, as well as for employees."

"When we see and hear our people proposing changes because the old way of doing things is not up to the new standards, we will know everyone is committed to the changes. That's an exciting prospect."

In short, everyone in the company — senior as well as junior staff — has to be committed to doing things right the first time.

In this company senior management and staff have started the process of identifiying individual requirements for doing things right the first time: they are committed to a long-term program for quality improvement.

Experience Number Two: Maintaining a Program

Armstrong World Industries Canada Limited is now in its fifth year of a quality improvement program. Kenneth Matheson, president, talked with me about their experience.

> All senior management attended introductory seminars prior to introducing the quality improvement program to the company. Then, as we got the program moving, we found that there was nothing earth shattering about it.

He emphasized that senior management must be "one hundred percent sold on the idea, and willing to communicate that commitment to employees."

He explained that staff were asked what had to be done to ensure that requirements are met every time a function is performed. They were also asked to identify who supplies what and to whom.

> We trained our white-collar people in the application of the philosophy of zero defects [things done right the first time]. We asked everyone to measure their performance of one area, to chart it over a period of time, and to come up with the means of making their performance perfect each time.

A recognition program is in place. Outstanding performers are rewarded through the introduction of both non-monetary recognition programs as well as monetary awards. The non-monetary winners are determined by peer groups. The monetary awards are presented on an ad hoc basis by managers and general managers.

> We keep emphasizing that our people are the Company, that their performance to a zero defect level makes us more successful, and that the more successful the Company is, the more secure are both their future and economic well-being.

As the program has progressed and evolved, senior management have begun to see the effect on individual employees and are very impressed with the positive changes that have taken place. This year, the program will be extended to plant employees. The idea of "zero defects" at the plant level has staggering bottom-line implications.

Matheson concludes: "Our aim is to do things right the first time, every time, in everything we do to run our business. Our corporate culture is changing to reflect this. We feel that we are a class act. We want to remain that way. To do so, we just have to have zero defects."

Your Service Improvement Program

You are committed to implementing a service program. Now, where do you start? Begin by looking at your own ideas of what a service improvement program is, as well as what a service improvement program would mean in your company or department.

Any service improvement program will fizzle and die if senior people:

• Do not plan and organize the program on paper,

outlining key steps in the process.

- Are not willing to invest time and financial resources in the program.
- Are not seen by staff to be active participants.
- Are perceived to be "telling us one more thing we have to do."
- Do not recognize the achievements and contributions of staff.
- Regard the program as a "Quick Fix."

Remember: Bridging the gap between intent and implementation requires much thought and planning at the senior level. But above everything else, senior management must have *absolute belief* in the goals as well as *commitment to participating* in the process.

Summary

1. Customers' essential service requirements are: predictability, consistency, reliability, fairness, continuity, and stability.

2. A service improvement program is long term and requires a high degree of energy, enthusiasm, and commitment from all levels of the organization. The corporate culture will reflect this enthusiasm and commitment.

3. A service improvement program begins with a fundamental operating principle. All operating policies must be congruent with this principle.

4. A company's service is a reflection of individual attitudes and behaviors at every level of the organization. The goal of quality service is achieved only when staff at all levels understand, accept and implement the

company's service principle and policies. Staff must be familiar with the principles and policies.

5. Bridging the gap between intent and implementation requires much thought and planning at the senior level. Senior management must have a common understanding of and absolute belief in the goals of the improvement program, and be committed to taking an active part in the program.

Take a Break... Time Out

DEFINING A SERVICE IMPROVEMENT PROGRAM:
TAKE THE QUIZ
This quiz was used to introduce ideas and initiate discussion about a service improvement program. You may find it useful for this purpose.

1. Service improvement is something you can put into place over the next few months, and then forget once you have reached your goal.   T   F

2. Service is the responsibility of specific people or departments.   T   F

3. Service standards reflect management attitudes and behavior.   T   F

4. Service improvement is a motivational program. T   F

5. Service improvement is a long range, attitude-changing plan.   T   F

6. Service improvement means that you tell people how to do things, such as how to be nice to customers.   T   F

7. Workers today are not interested in giving good service.   T   F

8. It is less costly to do things right the the first time than it is to correct errors.   T   F

9. Customers have unreasonable service demands. T   F

10. A service improvement program is expensive to
    implement.   T   F

All of these points have been covered throughout the
text, so the answers below are in summary form.

ANSWERS TO THE QUIZ

1. False. A service improvement program is never a quick
    fix. Lasting results are the outcome of a continuing
    emphasis on predetermined standards of performance
    for quality service.

2. False. Service is the responsibility of everyone in the
    organization. Senior management must be seen to be
    part of the service initiative.

3. True. Clearly defined service standards for everyone
    reflect managers' concern and commitment to the
    service program.

4. False. Service improvement depends on clearly de-
    fined standards of performance based on specific
    changes in behavior. Motivational exercises are part of
    an improvement program, but a program that relies
    solely on motivation — which is an emotional re-
    sponse — tends to fade away if it is not accompanied
    by specific behavior changes.

5. True. A goal of the long-range program is a change in
    attitude. You know you are succeeding when your
    employees become enthusiastic and eager to make
    changes and committed to putting the customer first.

6. False. A service improvement program means working
    with staff to provide appropriate training, not just
    telling them what to do. You cannot merely tell staff to
    behave in a certain way if you do not follow your own
    teaching. You and your staff must work together to
    identify aspects that need improvement and develop
    methods to implement changes.

7. False. Many workers today have never learned the

required skills. Managers must identify and teach service skills.

8. True. The time and other resources required to do everything right the first time are less than those needed to correct errors.

9. False. Identify the type of service you can offer and match this to the type of service your customers need.

10. False. A successful service improvement program requires commitment of financial and other resources but it should be considered an investment in the future of your business rather than a cost.

Take a Break... Time Out

A SUCCESSFUL IMPROVEMENT PROGRAM

As part of your service improvement program you need to ask these questions:

1. What does a staff person require to be able to do a specific job right the first time? Think in terms of skills, knowledge, and information from others in the company.

   This question can be used with any job, but it's interesting to apply this to front line "service" jobs such as garage attendants, receptionists, medical and hospital personnel, and hospitality staff. Social competency skills are high on the list of requirements in these areas.

2. What does it cost you *not* to meet any or some of those requirements?

   Again, this question is applicable to every area. Once you analyze this cost — loss of goodwill, loss of customer, time spent correcting errors, and handling complaints — you will see that eventually you always come up with dollars.

3. What is the cost of meeting requirements identified in question 1?

   Providing the service that you have identified as your standard has a cost, how does this cost compare when measured against question 2 above?

Appendix

Many people have kindly allowed me to use both their names and the names of their companies in stories and experiences that illustrate the important elements of quality service. These stories and experiences about every-day situations, by people who strive for — and attain — excellence, show that the fine art of service can be a reality. Below is a list of the people as well as a brief description of the companies mentioned in the book.

BARBARA CALDWELL is president of CleanWear Products, a company that manufactures disposable and expendable garments and accessories for hospitals, high tech and pharmaceutical companies, and general industry. Started by Barbara Caldwell in 1976, CleanWear employs 40 people and has sales of over $2 million annually.

LLOYD CRAWFORD is a district manager for the United Cooperatives of Ontario. This cooperative organization, owned by its members, employs about 1,300 full-time staff and has annual sales of $600 million.

JAMES GRAND is president of Grand & Toy Limited, a privately owned retail stationery and office supply company with 2,600 employees and 70 branches across the country.

BEN HARRISON is president of Metropolitan Insurance, a property and casualty insurance company, and a wholly owned subsidiary of Metropolitan Life. Metropolitan Insurance has 150 employees and annual sales in excess of $50 million.

RAY HOULD is executive vice president of All-Way Transportation Corporation, a school bus business which is a subsidiary of Vitran Corporation, a public company. All-Way, established in 1962, and taken over by present management in 1983, has over 1,000 employees, including management in 1983, has over 1,000 employees, including office staff and drivers, and annual revenue of $48 million.

KENNETH MATHESON is president of Armstrong World Industries Canada, privately owned by Armstrong World Industries Incorporated, U.S., which manufactures and sells hard surface resilient floor coverings and acoustical ceiling and wall materials. Armstrong World Industries Canada Limited was established in Canada in 1915, and now employs 725 people. Canadian sales are in excess of $1.25 million.

MIKE McELHONE is president of Interamerican Transport Systems Inc., a Canadian transportation sales and service company, active in both Canada and the United States. Interamerican has a staff of 27 and annual sales of $20 million.

JIM NICHOLSON is president of Paragon Industrial Photographic Reproductions Limited, where Don McRobb and Paul Overend give superb service. Paragon, established in 1957 and taken over by the new ownership in 1988, employs 65 people and has annual sales of $4–5 million.

RODD INNS, which includes the Grand Hotel, is a chain of inns and resorts in the Atlantic provinces, with a total of 8 properties, 700 rooms, and 700 employees. Mr. David Rodd is president of the company, which was established by his parents in Prince Edward Island in the early 1950s.

ROYAL DOULTON CANADA LIMITED, established in Canada in 1955, is a wholly owned subsidiary of Royal Doulton Limited in the United Kingdom. In Canada, Royal Doulton employs about 350 people and has annual sales in the $70 million range.

JERRY WEBSTER is director of Systems Integration Operations for Bull HN Information Systems Limited. Bull is a worldwide information systems company, serving over 50,000 customers in 28 countries, with revenues of $5 billion worldwide.

Index